The Plutarch Project Volume Three

(Revised)

Julius Caesar, Agis and Cleomenes, and the Gracchi

by

Anne E. White

ISBN: 978-1-990258-06-0

CONTENTS

Introduction i

Julius Caesar 1

    Lesson One 6

    Lesson Two 12

    Lesson Three 17

    Lesson Four 24

    Lesson Five 30

    Lesson Six 36

    Lesson Seven 42

    Lesson Eight 50

    Lesson Nine 57

    Lesson Ten 62

    Lesson Eleven 69

    Lesson Twelve 75

Agis and Cleomenes 84

    Lesson One 88

    Lesson Two 94

    Lesson Three 100

    Lesson Four 107

    Lesson Five 112

    Lesson Six 118

Lesson Seven...123

Lesson Eight...128

Lesson Nine..133

Lesson Ten..138

Lesson Eleven...143

Lesson Twelve..148

Tiberius and Gaius Gracchus..155

Lesson One...158

Lesson Two..163

Lesson Three..167

Lesson Four..173

Lesson Five..177

Lesson Six..182

Lesson Seven..187

Lesson Eight...192

Lesson Nine..197

Lesson Ten..202

Lesson Eleven...206

Lesson Twelve..212

Bibliography...218

About the Author..218

Introduction

These notes, and the accompanying text, are prepared for the use of individual students and small groups following a twelve-week term.

The text is a free mixture of Thomas North's 1579 translation of Plutarch's *Lives of the Noble Greeks and Romans* and John Dryden's 1683 translation. (Dryden for clarity, North for character.) Omissions have been made for length and suitability for the intended age group. Those using audio versions or other translations may want to preview those editions for similar "necessary omissions."

Using the Lesson Material

> "We do not tell the tales, we know we cannot, we read them as well as we know how and without comment, unless questions are asked. We rely upon the imagination of the children to work upon this material until it becomes theirs, and I think we do not deceive ourselves by so doing." (E.A. Parish in *The Parents' Review*)

Each study contains explanatory material before the first lesson. A little at the beginning may be useful to stir interest in the study, but it is not meant to be given all in one dose! I encourage you to make the lessons your own. Use the questions that are the most meaningful to you.

Some lessons are divided into two or three sections. These can be read all at once or used throughout the week.

Learning from the Examination Questions

One key to understanding Charlotte Mason's use of Plutarch's *Lives* can be found in the examination questions that were given. Something as innocent-sounding as Form III's "How did Alexander (the Great) spend his days at a time of leisure?" may end up being, as Charlotte would say, suggestive. There is nothing more there than a question-- but it's a thought-provoking one. Did Alexander make the dull time count for something, or was it unproductive? Form II's (younger students) were asked "Why and how did Alexander teach his men 'to acquaint themselves with hardness?'" Students were not being asked to write essays on the importance of fortitude, they were simply asked to recount what was said or done; but the idea was there, to be taken or not. In many cases the examination questions were based on a quotation, which suggests to teachers that we want to make sure such sayings are noticed and remembered, in whatever ways seem the most natural for us to do so. From Alexander again:

> "Alexander loved to remember and reward the worthy deeds of men."
> Give two instances in details,
> OR, "To live at pleasure is a vile thing, and to travail is princely."
> Why did Alexander thus rebuke his friends? Tell the whole story.

In the high school years, the quotations and the writing were at a higher level. From the Life of Julius Caesar, for Form IV (Grade 9):

> 1. Sketch briefly the character of Julius Caesar, and say to what events in his life the following sayings refer,--
>   (a), "A man can be but once undone, come on."
>   (b), "Time of war and law are two things."
>   (c), "Thou has Caesar and his fortune with thee."

And from Cleomenes, a question which seems to sum up much of Plutarch and Citizenship:

> What were some of the things that Cleomenes "thought most fit and honourable for a prince" in private and in public life?

The three studies here include possible questions for end-of-term examinations. The questions for Julius Caesar were adapted from original P.N.E.U. programmes. The others were written for this volume.

Julius Caesar
(100 B.C.— 44 B.C.)

Who Was Gaius Julius Caesar?

Julius Caesar was a Roman statesman and general in the first century B.C., the last years of the Republic. Over his long career, he held almost every high civic, military, and even religious position that existed. He was also a noted orator and writer. (An orator was a public speaker, usually someone who used those skills in political or legal matters.)

The Roman Republic (and small-e empire)

The Roman Empire did not formally exist until Octavius Caesar (later Caesar Augustus) became Emperor in 27 B.C. However, though it was still the era of the **Roman Republic**, Rome did have an empire because of the large amount of foreign territory it had acquired. For clarity, we will call it the small-e empire.

In the first century B.C., overseas conquests meant a great number of foreign captives; so small, family-run farms now competed with larger operations based on slave labour. The lack of small land owners forced the army to accept soldiers from the poorer classes, who then had to be paid more so that they could afford weapons. These soldiers considered themselves employees of the army (rather than citizens who occasionally had to fight): their loyalty was to their general, perhaps even more than to Rome itself.

Who were Sulla and Marius?

When Julius Caesar was about sixteen, a civil war began between two mighty Roman rivals: **Lucius Cornelius Sulla**, and Caesar's uncle-by-marriage, **Gaius Marius**, who was allied with another leader named **Lucius Cornelius Cinna**. Several personal events happened in Caesar's life at the same time: his father died, leaving him as head of the family; he nominated himself to be the High Priest of Jupiter (see the note below); and he was married to Cinna's daughter Cornelia. When Sulla's side gained power in Rome, Caesar (as a "Marian," or sympathizer with Marius) not only lost his position and inheritance, and was pressured to divorce his wife, but had to go into hiding as well. Even when the threat to his life ended, Caesar thought he would be safer away from Rome, so he joined military expeditions in Asia and Cilicia. It has been noted that that Rome was the real beneficiary of Caesar's "career change," since, as the High Priest of Jupiter (a special position that had many restrictions attached to it), he would not have been allowed to participate in the military.

A note on the spelling of Sulla: North and Dryden spell this name "Sylla," although other sources spell it "Sulla." The reason is that Plutarch wrote in Greek, and "Sylla" was his Greek version of the Latin name. I have used "Sulla" to avoid confusion.

Who were Caesar's wives?

As noted above, Caesar's first wife was Cornelia the daughter of Cinna; his second was Pompeia, the granddaughter of Sulla; and his third was Calpurnia, the one featured in Shakespeare's play. He was also engaged to another girl before his first marriage, but the rules of the priesthood required him to marry someone whose family was of equal rank to his.

What was the priesthood of Jupiter? What was the *Pontifex Maximus*?

Thomas North often used images from his own culture to translate Greek and Roman terms. Knights defended castles (forts); men opened their doublets and rode in carriages (chariots); and the high priest became a bishop. For our purposes, it is necessary only to know that there were numerous levels and types of priesthood in Rome and throughout the rest of Italy; and that these positions carried political as well as spiritual authority. Julius Caesar became a *pontifex* (priest) in 73 B.C., after the death of Sulla; and *Pontifex Maximus* (chief or high priest) in 63 B.C. These were different positions from that of High Priest of Jupiter, and did not keep him from military leadership.

What was an aedile, a quaestor, a consul?

The elected positions or magistracies in Rome were (starting at the bottom): quaestor, aedile, praetor, and consul. (The office of non-military tribune, or tribune of the people, was a separate position.) Ex-consuls could become censors, and a consul could become dictator if the need (usually a great emergency) arose.

What was a dictator?

In the early days of the Republic, **consuls** were sometimes suspected of taking office only so that they could bring back the monarchy. The office of *praetor maximus*, or **dictator**, was created as a safeguard: it gave the Romans the option of choosing someone who would act as the supreme magistrate of the city, and also as a military general during wartime, but for a limited period of time. Most Roman dictatorships took place during the first two hundred years of the Republic; the position became much less common in later times. Those who held the office of dictator in later years, such as Sulla and Julius Caesar, seemed to use it more for personal power, and this caused trouble.

Who were the tribunes?

The duty of a non-military **tribune** (sometimes called a tribune of the **plebeians**, or a "tribune of the people") was to protect the liberties of the common people from any individual or group (such as the nobles) who might take advantage of them or suppress their rights. This position was not part of the junior-senior ranking of **magistrates** such as **quaestor** and **consul**; it was an office voted on by the common people (**plebeians**), who themselves were bound by oath to protect the tribunes from harm.

Who were the Gauls and the Germans?

One of Julius Caesar's major contributions to the Roman Republic (soon to be the Roman Empire) was to enlarge its boundaries by taking over new territory in Europe. Throughout the story, we have the names of numerous tribes and sub-tribes, some of them Gauls, others Germans, but all of them seen as potential Roman soldiers/taxpayers. In Caesar's account of the Gallic Wars, the **Germans** were the various tribes who lived east of the **Rhine River**, and the **Gauls** were all those living to the west.

Who was Pompey?

Gnaeus Pompeius Magnus, or Pompey the Great, was a military and political leader, famous for his exploits in Sulla's Second Civil War. His marriage to Caesar's daughter Julia might have eased the rivalry between them, but her early death ended that possibility.

Who were all those other people whose names started with "C?"

Casca: Two Casca brothers were involved in the assassination of Caesar: **Publius Servilius Casca Longus**, who struck the first blow; and **Gaius Servilius Casca**, a close friend of Caesar**'s**.

Marcus Licinius Crassus, or **Crassus:** a Roman general and politician (115 B.C.-53 B.C.), one of the First Triumvirate with Caesar and Pompey; he was also known for his wealth.

Cassius: Gaius Cassius Longinus, a brother-in-law of Brutus, was a Roman senator and one of the conspirators against Caesar.

Cato: Marcus Porcius Cato Uticensis, or Cato the Younger, was a statesman who had frequent conflicts of opinion with Caesar.

Cicero: **Quintus Tullius Cicero** was a military leader during Caesar's Gallic wars. **Marcus Tullius Cicero**, his older brother, was a Roman statesman and orator, and was put to death in 43 B.C. because of his enmity to **Marcus Antonius**. (Because Shakespeare called Marcus Antonius by the anglicized Mark or Marc Antony, we often use that name as well.)

Cinna: there are several Cinnas in the story, beginning with **Lucius Cornelius Cinna (the Elder)**, Caesar's first father-in-law. Then we have **Lucius Cornelius Cinna (the Younger)**, one of the conspirators against Caesar; and **Helvius Cinna** or "Cinna the Poet," whose name led to an unfortunate misunderstanding.

Should we read Shakespeare's Julius Caesar at the same time?

In the original PNEU schools, students read William Shakespeare's play *The Tragedy of Julius Caesar* in the same term as Plutarch's *Life of Julius Caesar*. And why not? One lends interest to the other, and seeing what an expert dramatist created from the original source material is a wonderful lesson in writing. The problem with reading them at the same time is that the play focuses only on the last days of Caesar's life, with a shift at the end to Cassius and Brutus. If students are familiar with the story, they may not find it too confusing to jump so far ahead of their Plutarch readings. An alternative, not traditional for Charlotte Mason, but workable especially for younger students, might be to focus on Plutarch for the first part of the term; and then read the play. Notes on the play (Shakespeare Connections) are included in the last few lessons of this study.

Top Vocabulary Terms

1. **barbarians:** a general term referring here to non-Romans, particularly people of the northern tribes who seemed less "civilized" (or **barbarous**)

2. **clemency:** mercy, forgiveness. **Clementia** was the goddess of such virtues, and a Roman temple was dedicated to her (**Lesson Ten**).

3. **cohort:** A **cohort** was made up of about 480 soldiers.

4. **commonwealth:** a state (in this case Rome) and its dependencies, possessions, provinces and/or colonies

5. **corn:** grain, such as wheat or barley

6. **despise:** Not necessarily to dislike something or to find it disgusting ("I despise rutabagas"), but to regard something or someone with contempt, and possibly to underestimate it/them. "…despising a danger at first will make it at last irresistible" (**Lesson One**).

7. **foot:** "Foot" is another word for infantry, or foot soldiers. (The cavalry, or soldiers on horseback, is sometimes called just "horse.")

8. **The Forum:** also called **the marketplace**. The public place in Rome where speeches were made and business was carried out.

9. **legion:** a military unit made up (at that time) of about 4500 men

10. **magistrates:** elected officials

11. **mean:** Used several times as an adjective to mean insignificant, poor, inferior; of low social standing. **Means** can be a noun meaning a method or way of doing something ("he did not have the means to make it happen"). **Mean** is also used in its more usual verb sense ("what did she mean?").

12. **orator:** one who makes public speeches or **orations**.

13. **talent:** an amount of money, measured by its weight in gold or silver. The Roman talent was a third larger than the Athenian version, and about half the size of the talent mentioned in the New Testament; one Roman talent weighed just over 71 lb. (32.3 kg).

14. **triumph:** an official parade in celebration of a military victory

15. **victuals (pronounced "vittles"):** food supplies. It is occasionally used as a verb (to "victual" the soldiers).

Lesson One

Introduction

In a time when many in Rome were being put to death for their political loyalties (or even for being related to the wrong party), young

Julius Caesar was on the wrong side. Most people in that position would have stayed hidden or at least tried to live quietly; but Julius Caesar was never most people. In fact, he decided to put himself forward for the very public position of High Priest of Jupiter. General Sulla, who had recently won a civil war and become dictator of Rome, had been too busy to worry much about one teenage boy with Marian connections; but that got his attention, and now Caesar was in trouble.

Vocabulary

master: dictator (see introductory notes for this study)

put away: divorce

confiscating her dowry: taking away the money her family had paid to Caesar at their wedding

priesthood: see the introductory notes

he was yet a mere boy: Caesar was about eighteen

guards: not in the sense of prison guards, but rather as bodyguards, protecting his safety

hang them up: put them to death

discharged: freed

praetor: the office of praetor could include governorship of a province

the open house he kept: his hospitality

the whole state and commonwealth: the way things were governed

application: effort

Marius's exploits over the Cimbri: Sulla had taken the credit for this victory, and Caesar was now trying to give it back to his uncle.

extolled: praised

they that had him in estimation: his admirers

People

Sulla: Sulla was made Perpetual Dictator, but resigned after one year, and was elected as consul instead for 80 B.C., along with Metellus Pius, whom Caesar later replaced as *Pontifex Maximus*.

Cinna, Marius: see introductory notes for this study

King Nicomedes: Nicomedes IV Philopator, king of Bithynia from 94-74 B.C.

Marcus Juncus: governor of Asia in 75 B.C.

Historic Occasions

113-101 B.C.: Cimbrian War

106 B.C.: Birth of Pompey

100 B.C.: Birth of Julius Caesar

87 B.C.: Cinna and Marius took control in Rome

86 B.C.: Death of Marius

84 B.C.: Caesar married Cornelia

82/81 B.C.-79 B.C.: Sulla's dictatorship in Rome

78 B.C.: Death of Sulla

75 B.C.: Caesar kidnapped by pirates

70 B.C.: Pompey and Crassus were consuls together (the first time)

69 B.C.: Death of Cornelia

67 B.C.: Caesar returned from Spain and married Pompeia

On the Map

As an introduction to this study, it would be useful to examine a map of the Roman Republic and its surroundings in the first century B.C., including other lands which had become provinces, such as Spain and Syria. A map or pictures of Rome itself might also be helpful (what is meant by setting up statues in the Capitol?).

Other places mentioned in this lesson:

Cimbri: a tribe who were defeated in a war just before Caesar's birth

the country of the Sabines: a mountainous area northeast of Rome

Bithynia: a region in the northwestern part of **Asia Minor.** King Nicomedes IV (mentioned in the passage) died in 74 B.C. and bequeathed his kingdom to Rome, making it a province.

Pharmacusa: a small Greek island in the Aegean Sea

Cilicia (Cilicians): an ancient kingdom that is now part of Turkey

Miletus, Pergamum: Greek cities that are now part of Turkey

Rhodes: a Greek island which was famous as a center of learning

Reading

Part One

After **Sulla** became **master** of Rome, he wished to make Caesar **put away** his wife Cornelia, daughter of **Cinna**, the late sole ruler of the commonwealth; but was unable to effect it either by promises or intimidation, and so contented himself with **confiscating her dowry**. (The ground of Sulla's hostility to Caesar was the relationship between him and **Marius**. *[omission]*) And though at the beginning, while so many were to be put to death, and there was so much to do, Caesar was overlooked by Sulla; yet he would not keep quiet, but presented himself to the people as a candidate for the **priesthood**, though **he was yet a mere boy**. When Sulla was determined to have killed Caesar, some of his friends told him that it was to no purpose to put so young a boy as he to death. But Sulla answered that they knew little who did not see more than one Marius in that boy.

Caesar, understanding that, stole out of Rome, and hid himself a long time in **the country of the Sabines**, wandering still from place to place. But one day while moving from house to house, he fell into the hands of Sulla's soldiers, who searched all those places, and took them whom they found hidden. Caesar, by a bribe of two talents, prevailed with Cornelius, their captain, to let him go, and was no sooner dismissed but he put to sea and made for **Bithynia**. After a short stay there with **King Nicomedes**, in his passage back he was taken near the island of **Pharmacusa** by some of the pirates, who, at that time, with large fleets of ships and innumerable smaller vessels, infested the seas everywhere.

They asking him at the first twenty talents for his ransom, Caesar laughed them to scorn, as though they knew not what a man they had taken, and of himself promised them fifty talents. Then he sent his men up and down to get him this money, so that he was left in manner alone among these thieves of the **Cilicians** *[omission]*, with one of his friends, and two of his slaves only: and yet he made so little reckoning of them, that when he was desirous to sleep, he sent unto them to command them to make no noise.

For thirty-eight days he was not kept as a prisoner, but rather as a prince. He amused himself with joining in their exercises and games, as if they had not been his keepers, but his **guards**. And otherwhile also he would write verses, and make orations, and call them together to say them before them: and if any of them seemed as though they had not understood him, or passed not for them, he called them blockheads, and brute beasts, and laughing, threatened them that he would **hang them up**. But they were as merry with the matter as could be, and took all in good part, thinking that this his bold speech came through the simplicity of his youth.

As soon as his ransom was come from **Miletus**, he paid it, and was **discharged**; and proceeded at once to man some ships at the port of Miletus, and went in pursuit of the pirates, whom he surprised with their ships still stationed at the island; and took most of them. Their money he made his prize, and the men he secured in prison at **Pergamum**; and he made application to **Marcus Juncus**, who was then governor of Asia, whose duty it was, as **praetor**, to determine their punishment. Juncus, having his eye upon the money, for the sum was considerable, said he would think at his leisure what to do with the prisoners. Caesar leaving Juncus there, returned again unto Pergamum, and there hung up all these thieves openly upon a cross, as he had oftentimes promised them in the isle he would do, when they thought he did but jest.

Part Two

*[Omission: Caesar spent some time studying in **Rhodes**, and then returned to Rome. He became active in public life, taking cases as a lawyer.]*

Now Caesar immediately won many men's good wills at Rome, through his eloquence in pleading of their causes: and the people loved him marvellously also, in which he showed a tact and consideration beyond what could have been expected at his age; and **the open house he kept**, the entertainments he gave, and the general splendour of his manner of life contributed little by little to create and increase his political influence. His enemies slighted the growth of it at first, presuming it would soon fail when his money was gone; whilst in the meantime it was growing up and flourishing among the common people. But in fine, when they had thus given him the bridle to grow to this greatness, and that they could not then pull him back, and now openly tended to the altering of **the whole state and commonwealth** of Rome: too late they found that there is no beginning so mean, which continued **application** will not make considerable; and that despising a danger at first will make it at last irresistible.

Part Three

[Caesar became a tribune (72 B.C.) and then treasurer, or quaestor (68/67 B.C.), and aedile (65 B.C.). He lost his wife Cornelia, but then married again.]

At that time there were two factions in Rome, one that of Sulla, which was very powerful; the other that of Marius, which was then broken and in a very low condition; Caesar undertook to revive this and to make it his own. And to this end, whilst he was in the height of his repute with the people for the magnificent shows he gave as aedile, he ordered images of Marius and figures of Victory, with trophies in their hands, to be carried privately in the night and placed in the Capitol. Next morning when some saw them bright with gold and beautifully made, with inscriptions upon them, referring them to **Marius's**

exploits over the Cimbri, they were surprised at the boldness of him who had set them up; nor was it difficult to guess who it was.

Hereupon, it ran straight through all the city, and every man came thither to see them. Then some cried out upon Caesar, and said it was a tyranny which he meant to set up, by renewing of such honours as before had been trodden underfoot, and forgotten by common decree and open proclamation; and that it was no more but a bait to gauge the people's goodwill *[omission]*. On the other hand, Marius's party took courage, and it was incredible how numerous they were suddenly seen to be, and what a multitude of them appeared and came shouting into the Capitol. Many, when they saw Marius's likeness, cried for joy, and Caesar was highly **extolled** as the one man, in the place of all others, who was a relation worthy of Marius *[omission]*. Thereupon **they that had him in estimation** did grow in better hope than before, and persuaded him *[omission]* through the goodwill of the people, he should be better than all of them, and be first man in the commonwealth.

Narration and Discussion

What impressions do you have already of Julius Caesar?

"For thirty-eight days he was not kept as a prisoner, but rather as a prince." Give some examples.

For further thought: "Despising a danger at first will make it at last irresistible." This lesson seems to prove this in more ways than one. What is the danger in ignoring a small problem? Can you think of any Scriptures that support this? (Song of Solomon 2:15)

Creative narration: Write or act out a news story about the statues in the Capitol.

Lesson Two

Introduction

From quaestor and aedile to *Pontifex Maximus*, praetor, and finally consul: was there any higher that Caesar could go?

Vocabulary

high priest: *Pontifex Maximus* (see introductory notes).

most apprehensive of the event: most worried about the outcome

importunate: insistent that he pay back the money he owed them

usury: demanding excessive amounts of interest on loans

let the triumph fall: let it pass, drop it

assumed a policy: devised a strategy

People

Catulus: Quintus Lutatius Catulus Capitolinus, a politician who was an avowed enemy to the Marian party. (His father, also named Catulus, had fallen out with Marius over the Cimbri issue (**Lesson One**) and had become a supporter of Sulla; but when Marius came to power in 87 B.C., he committed suicide rather than be executed for disloyalty.)

Isauricus (#1): a consul (79 B.C.) and general who was known for fighting against the Cilician pirates. He was the father of the **Isauricus (#2)** who was co-consul with Caesar in 48 B.C.

Crassus, Cato: see introductory notes

Alexander: Alexander the Great

Calpurnius Bibulus: Marcus Calpurnius Bibulus, the unfortunate politician who was elected consul along with Caesar for 59 B.C.

Historic Occasions

63 B.C.: Caesar became *Pontifex Maximus*

62 B.C.: Caesar served as praetor and governor of Spain

61 B.C.: Caesar divorced his wife Pompeia

60 B.C.: Caesar was elected consul for the following year (59 B.C.)

On the Map

Spain(s): Spain was divided into two provinces, Near and Far Spain.

Callaici: or Gallaeci; a group of tribes living in the **Iberian Peninsula**

Lusitani: or Lusitanians; a tribe of the Iberian Peninsula

Reading

Part One

At that time, Metellus the **high priest** died, and **Catulus** and **Isauricus**, persons of the highest reputation, and who had great influence in the Senate, were competitors for the office; yet Caesar would not give way to them, but presented himself to the people as a candidate against them. The several parties seeming very equal, Catulus, who, because he had the most honour to lose, was the **most apprehensive of the event**, sent to Caesar to buy him off, with offers of a great sum of money. But his answer was that he was ready to borrow a larger sum than that to carry on the contest.

When the day of the election came, his mother bringing him to the door of his house, Caesar weeping, kissed her, and said, "Mother, today you will see me either high priest or an exile." In fine, when the voices of the people were gathered together, and the strife well debated, Caesar won the victory, and made the Senate and noblemen all afraid of him: for that they thought that thenceforth he would make the people do what he thought good.

Part Two

[Omission: Caesar made some powerful enemies during the Catiline Conspiracy crisis, when he argued against putting criminals of noble families to death. He then prepared to go to Spain to take up the office of governor there.]

Caesar, in the meantime *[omission]*, had got the province of Spain, but was in great embarrassment with his creditors, who, as he was going off, came upon him, and were very pressing and **importunate**. This led him to apply himself to **Crassus**, who was the richest man in Rome, and that stood in need of Caesar's boldness and courage *[Dryden: youthful vigour and heat]* to withstand Pompey's greatness in the commonwealth. Crassus took upon him to satisfy those creditors who were most uneasy to him, and would not be put off any longer; and engaged himself to the amount of eight hundred and thirty talents; upon which Caesar was now at liberty to go to his province.

In his journey, as he was crossing the Alps, and passing by a small village of the barbarians with but few inhabitants, and those wretchedly poor, his companions asked the question among themselves, by way of mockery, if there were any contending for offices in that town, and whether there were any strife there amongst the noblemen for honour. To which Caesar made answer seriously, "For my part, I had rather be the chiefest man here, than the second person in Rome."

Another time also when he was in Spain, reading the history of **Alexander's** acts, when he had read it, he was sorrowful a good while after, and then burst out in weeping. His friends, seeing that, marvelled what should be the cause of his sorrow. "Do ye not think," said he, "that I have good cause to be heavy, when King Alexander being no older than myself is now, had in old time won so many nations and countries; and that I hitherunto have done nothing worthy of myself?"

Therefore when he was come into Spain, he was very careful of his business, and had in few days joined ten new cohorts of foot in addition to the twenty which were there before. With these he marched against the **Calaici** and **Lusitani**, and conquered them; and advancing as far as the ocean, subdued the tribes which never before had been subject to the Romans.

There he took order for pacifying of the war, and did as wisely take order for the establishing of peace. For he did reconcile the cities together, and made them friends one with another, but specially he pacified all suits of law, and strife betwixt the debtors and creditors, which had grown by reason of **usury**. For he ordained that the creditors should take yearly two parts of the revenue of their debtors, until such time as they had paid themselves; and that the debtors should have the third part to themselves to live withal. This conduct made him leave his province with a fair reputation; being rich himself, and having enriched his soldiers, and having received from them the honourable name of *Imperator*, or "sovereign captain."

Part Three

[Caesar now had a problem. He was in line for a military triumph, but he also wanted to run for consul, and the rules for the two contradicted each other.]

Now the Romans had a custom that such as demanded the honour of triumph should remain awhile outside the city; and that they, on the other side, which sued for the consulship, should of necessity be there in person. Caesar coming unhappily at that very time when the consuls were chosen, he sent to pray the Senate to do him that favour, that being absent, he might by his friends sue for the consulship. **Cato** at the first did protest against it, vouching an express law forbidding the contrary. But afterwards, perceiving that, notwithstanding the reasons he alleged, many of the senators (being won by Caesar) favoured his request: yet he cunningly sought all he could to prevent and delay them. Caesar thereupon determined rather to let the triumph fall, and to make suit for the consulship.

Entering the town and coming forward immediately, he **assumed a policy** by which everybody was deceived but Cato. This was the reconciling of Crassus and Pompey, the two men who then were most powerful in Rome. There had been a quarrel between them, which he now succeeded in making up, and by this means he strengthened himself by the united power of both; and so under the cover of an action which carried all the appearance of a piece of kindness and good-nature, he caused what was, in effect, a revolution in the government. For it was not the quarrel between Pompey and Caesar, as most men imagine, which was the origin of the civil wars; but their union, their conspiring together at first to subvert the aristocracy, and so quarreling afterwards between themselves. Cato, who often foretold what the consequence of this alliance would be, had then the character of a sullen, interfering man; but in the end the reputation of a wise but unsuccessful counsellor.

Thus Caesar, being doubly supported by the interests of Crassus and Pompey, was promoted to the consulship, along with **Calpurnius Bibulus**.

Narration and Discussion

Caesar said, "For my part, I had rather be the chiefest man here, than the second person in Rome." What did he mean?

Discuss Caesar's reaction to his reading of Alexander. Should the stories of heroes make us weep?

Why was Caesar's reconciliation of Pompey and Crassus actually a play for power? Can peacemaking ever be a bad or a selfish thing?

Creative narration: Tell the story of the election from the point of view of a) Catulus or b) Caesar's mother.

Lesson Three

Introduction

The year 59 B.C. was referred to afterwards as the "Consulship of Julius and Caesar." In this political soap opera, alliances between the heavyweights alternated with smear campaigns and backstabbing. By the end of the year, Caesar was badly in need of something that would regain the Romans' trust and respect. (A war might work.)

What ailed Caesar?

Because of Plutarch's comments, there is a belief that Julius Caesar had "the falling sickness," or epilepsy. However, scholars have not agreed on what sort of seizures or spells of weakness he had, or what caused them.

Vocabulary

preferred: proposed

division of lands: a redistribution of land that would benefit veteran soldiers

gratis: free

such a colourable pretext: such a wonderful excuse

overhardness and austerity: strict, miserly policies

one on each side: as a declaration that they had teamed up together

target: shield

vehemence: energetic fury

contracted: engaged (by arrangement between the families)

that had offered his wife such dishonour: see note under **People**

perfidiousness: disloyalty, treachery

conciliated: pacified; gained their esteem and goodwill

wantonness: wild behaviour

liberal: generous

pricked him forward: motivated him, urged him

subject to headache…: see note on this (above)

a pretext for his ease: an excuse for taking things easy

physic: medicine

indefatigable: untiring

lodging in the field: sleeping outdoors

by writing ciphers in letters: the Roman writer Suetonius wrote this
about Caesar: "… if he had anything confidential to say, he wrote it in
cipher, that is, by so changing the order of the letters of the alphabet,
that not a word could be made out." This type of substitution cipher
is still called a Caesar Cipher.

sweet ointment: also translated "oil of perfume" or "myrrh." It appears
that Valerius Leo hadn't just pulled out the wrong bottle of salad
dressing, rather that he was trying to show off his wealth. The

reference to the host's **want of breeding** seems to confirm that.

People

(Quintus) Servilius Caepio: There were various Romans by this name, but none of them seem to have been engaged to Caesar's daughter **Julia**. Some have suggested that it might refer to Brutus, who went by that name at one time.

Piso: Lucius Calpurnius Piso Caesoninus (c. 100 BC – 43 BC), consul in 58 B.C. He is known for his antagonism to **Marcus Tullius Cicero**.

Clodius: Publius Clodius Pulcher. Clodius had "gate-crashed" a women's religious ritual at Julius Caesar's house, which was a serious matter and caused Caesar to divorce his wife Pompeia.

Historic Occasions

59 B.C.: Caesar was consul

59 B.C.: Caesar married his third wife, Calpurnia

On the Map

Gaul: see introductory notes for this study

Illyricum (Illyrians): a region of southeastern Europe

Massilia: the city of Marseilles, in France

Córdoba: a city in southern Spain

Rhône: a major river of Europe (not to be confused with the Rhine)

Milan: a large city in Italy

Reading

Part One

When Caesar entered into the office of consul, he brought in bills which would have been **preferred** with better grace by the most audacious of the tribunes, than by a consul; in which he proposed **the division of lands**, and distributing of corn to every citizen **gratis**, simply to please the common people. The best and most honourable of the senators opposed it; upon which, as he had long wished for nothing more than for **such a colourable pretext**, he loudly protested that by the **overhardness and austerity** of the Senate, they drove him against his will to lean unto the people.

And so he hurried out of the Senate, and presenting himself to the people, and there placing Crassus and Pompey **one on each side** of him, he asked the two of them whether they consented to the bills he had proposed. They both answered, they did. Then he prayed them to stand by him against those that had threatened to oppose him with their swords. Crassus gave him his word, he would. Pompey also did the like, and added thereunto that he would come with his sword and **target** both, against them that would withstand him with their swords. These words the nobles much resented, as neither suitable to his own dignity, nor becoming the reverence due to the Senate, but resembling rather the **vehemence** of a boy or the fury of a madman. But the people were pleased with it.

In order to get a yet firmer hold upon Pompey, Caesar having a daughter, **Julia**, who had been before **contracted** to **Servilius Caepio**, now betrothed her to Pompey, and told Servilius he should have Pompey's daughter, who was not unengaged either, but promised to Sulla's son Faustus. A little time after, Caesar married Calpurnia, the daughter of **Piso**, and got Piso made consul for the year following. Cato exclaimed loudly against this, and protested, with a great deal of warmth, that it was a shameful matter, and not to be suffered, that they should in that sort make havoc of the empire of Rome, distributing among themselves, through those wicked marriages, the governments of the provinces, and of great armies.

Calpurnius Bibulus, fellow consul with Caesar, perceiving that he did contend in vain, making all the resistance he could to withstand this law, and that oftentimes he was in danger to be slain with Cato, in the Forum and assembly: he kept close in his house all the rest of his consulship. Pompey, when he was married, at once filled the Forum with soldiers, and gave the people his help in passing the new laws, and secured Caesar the government of all **Gaul**, both on this and the other side of the Alps, together with **Illyricum**, and the command of four legions for five years.

Cato made some attempts against these proceedings, but was seized and led off on the way to prison by Caesar, who expected that he would appeal to the tribunes. But when he saw that Cato went along without speaking a word, and not only the nobility were indignant, but the people also, out of respect for Cato's virtue, were following in silence, and with dejected looks, he himself secretly did pray one of the tribunes that he would take Cato from the officers *[omission]*.

But the most disgraceful thing that was done in Caesar's consulship was his assisting to gain the tribuneship for the same **Clodius that had offered his wife such dishonour**, and profaned the holy ancient mysteries of the women, which were celebrated in his own house. He was elected on purpose to effect Cicero's downfall; nor did Caesar leave the city to join his army till they two had overpowered Cicero and driven him out of Italy.

Part Two

Thus far we have followed Caesar's actions before the wars of Gaul. After this, he seems to begin his course afresh, and to enter upon a new life and scene of action. And the period of those wars which he now fought, and those many expeditions in which he subdued Gaul, showed him to be a soldier and general not in the least inferior to any of the greatest and most admired commanders who had ever appeared at the head of armies.

For whosoever would compare the house of the Fabians, of the Scipios, of the Metellians, yea those also of his own time, or long before him, as Sulla, Marius, the two Lucullians, and Pompey himself, whose fame ascendeth up unto the heavens: but it will appear that Caesar's skill and his deeds of arms did excel them all together. One he may be held to have outdone in consideration of the difficulty of the country in which he fought, another in the extent of territory which he conquered; some, in the number and strength of the enemy whom he defeated; one man, because of the wildness and **perfidiousness** of the tribes whose goodwill he **conciliated**, another in his humanity and clemency to those he overpowered; others, again, in his gifts and kindnesses to his soldiers; all alike in the number of the battles which he fought and the enemies whom he killed. For he had not pursued the wars in Gaul full ten years when he had taken by storm above eight hundred towns, subdued three hundred states, and of the three millions of men, who made up the gross sum of those with whom at several times he engaged, he had killed one million and taken captive a second.

He was so much master of the goodwill and hearty service of his soldiers, that those who in other expeditions were but ordinary men displayed a courage past defeating or withstanding when they went upon any danger where Caesar's glory was concerned. And this appeareth plainly by the example of Acilius: who in a battle by sea before the city of **Massilia**, boarding one of his enemies' ships, one cut off his right hand with a sword, but yet he forsook not his target which he had in his left hand, but thrust it in his enemies' faces, and made them flee, so that he won their ship from them.

[Omission for length]

Part Three

Now Caesar himself did breed this noble courage and life in them. First, for that he gave them bountifully, and did honour them also, showing thereby that he did not heap up riches in the wars to maintain his life afterwards in **wantonness** and pleasure, but that he did keep it in store, honourably to reward their valiant service: and that by so much he thought himself rich, by how much he was **liberal** in rewarding of them that had deserved it.

Furthermore, they did not wonder so much at his valiantness in putting himself at every instant in such manifest danger, and in taking so extreme pains as he did, knowing that it was his greedy desire of honour that set him afire, and **pricked him forward** to do it: but that he always continued all labour and hardness, more than his body could bear, that filled them all with admiration. For he was a spare man, had a soft and pale skin, and was often **subject to headache, and otherwise to the falling sickness**: (the which took him the first time, as it is reported, in **Córdoba**). But he did not make the weakness of his constitution **a pretext for his ease**, but rather used war as the best **physic** against his indispositions; whilst, by **indefatigable** journeys, coarse diet, frequent **lodging in the field**, and continual laborious exercise, he struggled with his diseases, and fortified his body against all attacks.

He slept generally in his chariots or litters, employing even his rest in pursuit of action. In the day he was thus carried to the forts, garrisons, and camps, one servant sitting with him, who used to write down what he dictated as he went, and a soldier attending behind him with his sword drawn. He drove so rapidly that when he first left Rome he arrived at the river **Rhône** within eight days. He had been an expert rider from his childhood; for it was usual with him to sit with his hand joined together behind his back, and so to put his horse to its full speed. In his wars in Gaul, he did further exercise himself to dictate letters as he rode by the way, and did occupy two secretaries at once with as much as they could write; and as Oppius writeth, more than two at a time.

And it is reported, that Caesar was the first that devised friends might talk together **by writing ciphers in letters**, when he had no leisure to speak with them for his urgent business, and for the great distance besides from Rome.

Sidebar: Caesar's Generous Side

How little account Caesar made of his diet, this example doth prove it. When at the table of Valerius Leo, who entertained him at the supper at **Milan**, a dish of asparagus was put before him on which his host instead of salad oil had poured **sweet ointment**. Caesar partook of it without any disgust, and reprimanded his friends for finding fault with it. "For it was enough," said he, "not to eat what you did not like; but he who reflects on another man's **want of breeding** shows he wants it as much himself."

Another time upon the road he was driven by a storm into a poor man's cottage, where he found but one room, and that such as would afford but a mean reception to a single person, and therefore told his companions that places of honour should be given up to the greater men, and necessary accommodations to the weaker; and accordingly ordered that Oppius, who was in bad health, should lodge within, whilst he and the rest slept under a shed at the door.

Narration and Discussion

Tell two things that you admire about Julius Caesar so far, and one thing that you do not.

How did Caesar show himself an expert on time management as well as dinner-party etiquette?

Plutarch seems to jump quickly from Caesar's negative experience as consul to his career as (in North's words) "the wisest and most valiantest general." Should later success allow us to forget someone's earlier mistakes or misdeeds?

For further thought: "Now Caesar himself did breed this noble courage and life in them." North's words are actually "Caesar self did breed…", which seems to put the emphasis on Caesar's character, pointing more at what he was than at what he did. How did Caesar (in either sense) "breed noble courage and life" into his soldiers?

Lesson Four

Introduction

"All Gaul is divided into three parts, one of which the Belgae inhabit, the Aquitani another, and those who in their own language are called Celts, in ours Gauls, the third. All these differ from each other in language, customs and laws." **This is the famous beginning of *The Gallic Wars*, by Julius Caesar. The war for European control was a long, expensive gamble, but one that promised large returns.**

Vocabulary

confederates: allies

break their strength: break down their fortification

in defense of the Gauls against the Germans: This is a bit of a contentious issue for historians, but the basic idea is that Caesar, having so many victories over the Gauls, claimed them for the Romans, and therefore wanted to "protect" them against the even more "barbaric" tribes across the Rhine.

two hundred furlongs: A furlong is an eighth of a mile, so 200 furlongs would be 25 miles (about 40 km).

in consternation: disturbed, even frantic

intimation: news, information

expedient to attack them…: a good idea to attack while they were still frightened

stronghold: fort

galled and fretted them: made them so angry

spoils: treasure or loot taken after a raid or a battle

expedition: speed

eminent: notable, prominent

lictors: bodyguards who carried the "rods and axes" or *fasces*, a symbol of Roman power

seasonably: in a timely manner

People

Labienus: Titus Labienus, tribune of the people in 63 B.C.; one of Caesar's lieutenants in the Gallic Wars; but he supported Pompey during the civil war, and was killed at the Battle of Munda.

Ariovistus: the leader of the **Suebi** (or Suevi) people. The Suebi were a group of Germanic tribes originally from the River Elbe region.

Historic Occasions

58 B.C.: Beginning of the Gallic Wars

56 B.C: Meeting at Lucca

55 B.C.: Pompey and Crassus were consuls together (the second time)

55 B.C.: Caesar built a bridge across the Rhine, and invaded Britain

On the Map

Gauls, Germans: see introductory notes for this study

Helvetians: or Helvetii; a Celtic tribe occupying the Swiss plateau. The **Tigurini** were a subgroup of this tribe.

Teutones: a tribe who had fought the Romans along with the **Cimbri**

Rhine: the second-longest river in Europe

country of the Sequani: a tribe living on the **Arar River** (the Saône).

Po (river): the longest river in Italy, flowing eastward across northern Italy to the Adriatic Sea.

Rubicon: a river in northeastern Italy which served as the boundary between Cisalpine Gaul and Italy itself.

Belgae: tribes living in northern **Gaul**, which included the **Nervii**

Lucca: a city in the region of Tuscany, in central Italy

Reading

Part One

The first war that Caesar made with the Gauls was with the **Helvetians** and **Tigurini**, who having set fire of all their good cities, twelve in number, and four hundred villages besides, would have marched forward through that part of Gaul which was included in the Roman province, as the Cimbri and **Teutones** formerly had done. Nor were they inferior to these in courage; and in numbers they were equal, being in all three hundred thousand, of which one hundred and ninety thousand were fighting men. Caesar did not engage the Tigurini in person, but **Labienus**, under his directions, routed them near the **river Arar**.

But the Helvetians themselves came suddenly with their army to set upon him, as he was going towards a city of his **confederates**. Caesar perceiving that, made haste to get him to some place of strength, and there did set his men in battle array. When one brought him his horse to get up on which he used in battle, he said unto them: "When I have overcome mine enemies, I will then get up on him to follow the chase, but now let us give them charge."

Therewith he marched forward afoot, and gave charge: and there fought it out a long time, before he could make them flee that were in battle. But the greatest trouble he had, was to distress their camp, and to **break their strength** which they had made with their carts. For there they, that before had fled from the battle, did not only put themselves in force, and valiantly fought it out; but their wives and children, also fighting for their lives to the death, were all slain, and the battle was scant ended at midnight.

Now if the act of this victory was famous, unto that he also added another as notable, or exceeding it. For of all the barbarous people that had escaped from this battle, he gathered together again above a hundred thousand of them, and compelled them to return home into their country which they had forsaken, and unto their towns also which they had burnt: this he did for fear the **Germans** should pass it and possess themselves of the land whilst it lay uninhabited.

Part Two

The second war he made was **in defense of the Gauls against the Germans**: although before, he himself had caused **Ariovistus**, their king, to be received for an ally of the Romans. Notwithstanding, they were grown very unquiet neighbours, and it appeared plainly that, having any occasion offered them to enlarge their territories, they would not content them with their own, but meant to invade and possess the rest of Gaul. Caesar, perceiving that some of his captains trembled for fear, but especially the young gentlemen of noble houses of Rome, who thought to have gone to the wars with him as only for their pleasure and gain: he called them to council, and commanded them that were afraid, that they should depart home, and not put themselves in danger against their wills, since they had such weak and faint hearts to shrink when he had need of them. And for himself, he said, he would set upon the barbarous people, even if he had left him but the Tenth Legion only, saying that the enemies were no valianter than the Cimbri had been, nor that he (Caesar) was a captain inferior unto Marius. This oration being made, the soldiers of the Tenth Legion sent their lieutenants unto him, to thank him for the good opinion he had of them; and the other legions also fell out with their captains, and all of them together followed him many days' journey with goodwill to serve him, until they came within **two hundred furlongs** of the camp of the enemies.

Ariovistus's courage to some extent was cooled upon their very approach; for never expecting the Romans would attack the Germans, whom he had thought it more likely they would not venture to withstand even its defense of their own subjects, he was the more surprised at Caesar's conduct, and saw his army to be **in consternation.** They were still more discouraged by the prophecies of their holy women, who foretell the future by observing the eddies of rivers, and taking signs from the windings and noise of streams; and who now warned them not to engage before the next new moon appeared.

Caesar having had **intimation** of this, and seeing the Germans lie still, thought it **expedient to attack them whilst they were under these apprehensions**, rather than sit still and wait their time. Accordingly, he made his approaches to the **strongholds** and hills on which they lay encamped, and so **galled and fretted them** that at last they came down with great fury to engage. But he gained a signal victory, and pursued them for four hundred furlongs, as far as the **Rhine**; all which space was covered with **spoils** and bodies of the slain. Ariovistus made shift to pass the Rhine with the small remains of an army, for it is said the number of the slain amounted to eighty thousand.

Part Three

After this action, Caesar left his army at their winter quarters in the **country of the Sequani**, and, in order to attend to affairs at Rome, went into that part of Gaul which lies on the **Po**, and was part of his province; for the river **Rubicon** divides Gaul, which is on this side the Alps, from the rest of Italy. There he sat down and employed himself in courting people's favour; great numbers coming to him continually, and always finding their requests answered; for he never failed to dismiss all with present pledges of his kindness in hand, and further hopes for the future.

And during all this time of the war in Gaul, Pompey never observed how Caesar was on the one hand using the arms of Rome to effect his conquests, and on the other was gaining over and securing to himself the favour of the Romans with the wealth which those conquests obtained him. But when he heard that the **Belgae**, who were the most powerful of all the Gauls, and inhabited a third part of the country, were revolted, and had got together a great many thousand men in arms, he immediately set out and took his way hither with great **expedition**, and falling upon the enemy as they were ravaging the Gauls, his allies, he soon defeated and put to flight the largest and least scattered division of them. For though their numbers were great, yet they made but a slender defense, and the marshes and deep rivers were made passable to the Roman foot by the vast quantity of dead bodies.

*[Omission for length: Caesar's army fought a bloody battle against the **Nervii**, a particularly fierce tribe. There were many casualties on both sides, but the Romans won, and there were great celebrations back in Rome.]*

Part Four

For when Caesar had set his affairs at a stay in Gaul, on the other side of the Alps: he always used to lie about the Po River in the wintertime, to give direction for the establishing of things at Rome, at his pleasure. All who were candidates for offices used his assistance, and were supplied with money from him to corrupt the people and buy their votes, in return of which, when they were chosen, they did all things to advance his power. But what was more considerable, the most **eminent** and powerful men in Rome in great numbers came to visit him at **Lucca**: Pompey, and Crassus, and Appius, the governor of Sardinia, and Nepos, the proconsul of Spain; so that there were in the place at one time one hundred and twenty **lictors** and more than two hundred senators.

There they fell in consultation, and determined that Pompey and Crassus should again be chosen consuls the next year following. Furthermore, they did appoint that Caesar should have money again delivered him to pay his army, and besides, did extend the time of his government five years further. This was thought a very strange and an unreasonable matter unto wise men. For they themselves that had taken so much money of Caesar, persuaded the Senate to let him have money of the common treasure, as though he had had none before: yea to speak more plainly, they compelled the Senate unto it, sighing and lamenting to see the decrees they passed. Cato was not present, for they had sent him **seasonably** out of the way into Cyprus; but Favonius, who was a zealous imitator of Cato, when he found he could do no good by opposing it, broke out of the house, and loudly declaimed against these proceedings to the people, but none gave him any hearing; some slighting him out of respect to Crassus and Pompey, and the greater part to gratify Caesar, on whom depended their hopes.

Narration and Discussion

Why was the Roman Senate now more willing to grant Caesar money and other favours (even if the proposal came from his friends)?

Creative narration #1: Write or act out the scene, including Caesar's speech to his men, before the fight with Ariovistus.

Creative narration #2: You are a student, of any era, and you have to read the beginning of *Caesar's Gallic Wars* for homework; but you don't understand what it is about. Write, act out, or otherwise create a conversation between yourself and someone (such as a grandparent) who can enlighten you.

Lesson Five

Introduction

Caesar continued his military adventures in Gaul, but was somewhat disappointed by not finding much financial reward in fighting against barbarous peoples. At this time, he also received the news that his daughter Julia, Pompey's wife, had died in childbirth. When the Roman army had been divided into garrisons for the wintertime, and Caesar was in Italy, the Gauls rebelled against him again. But this time, fate seemed to favour the Romans.

Vocabulary

outbreak: rebellion

ramparts: defensive walls

heighten the enemy's contempt of them: the plan was to make the enemy think they were weaker than they really were

he issued forth: the soldiers behind the walls charged out at the enemy

levied: collected, gotten together

invincible: unconquerable

post or courier: messenger

myriad: a military unit of ten thousand soldiers

impregnable: unable to be broken through or captured

plate and moveables: treasure, such as silver cups

caparison and furniture: a horse's ornamental covering and harness

People

Ambiorix: or Abriorix, the leader of the Eburones, a tribe of northeastern Gaul

Cotta and **Titurius:** Lucius Aurunculeius Cotta and Quintus Titurius Sabinus

Quintus Tullius Cicero: Brother of Marcus Tullius Cicero (see introductory notes)

Vercingetorix: the king of the **Arverni** tribe, captured at the **Battle of Alesia**

Historic Occasions

53 B.C.: the death of Crassus

53 B.C.: Gnaeus Domitius Calvinus (#2) was consul (**Lesson Eight**)

52 B.C.: the Battle of Alesia

52 B.C.: Vercingetorix surrendered to Rome (He was held in prison until Caesar's triumph in 46 B.C., and then executed.)

On the Map

Arverni: or Arvenians; those who lived in what is now the Auvergne region of France

Carnutini: also called the Carnutes or Carnuti, meaning "the horned ones"; a tribe living between the Sequana (Seine) and Liger (Loire) rivers in what is now France

Aedui: a Gallic tribe who lived in the region of France now called Burgundy

country of the Ligones: believed to be the Emilia-Romagna region of northern Italy

Alesia: a town believed to be in Burgundy (there is some controversy about its location)

Reading

Part One

Caesar's army was now grown very numerous, so that he was forced to disperse them into various camps for their winter quarters; and he having gone himself to Italy as he used to do, in his absence a general **outbreak** throughout the whole of Gaul commenced, and large armies marched about the country, and attacked the Roman quarters, and attempted to make themselves masters of the forts where they lay.

The greatest and strongest party of the rebels, under the command of **Ambiorix**, cut off **Cotta** and **Titurius** with all their men, while a force sixty thousand strong besieged the legion under the command of **Quintus Tullius Cicero**, and had almost taken it by storm, the Roman soldiers being all wounded, and having quite spent themselves by a defense beyond their natural strength. But Caesar, who was at a great distance, having received the news, quickly got together seven thousand men, and hastened to relieve Cicero. The besiegers were aware of it, and went to meet him, with great confidence that they should easily overpower such a handful of men.

Caesar, to deceive them, still drew back and made as though he fled from them, lodging in places meet for a captain that had but a few to fight with a great number of his enemies. He commanded his men in no wise to stir out to skirmish with them, but compelled them to raise up the **ramparts** of his camp, and to fortify the gates, that by show of fear they might **heighten the enemy's contempt of them**. Till at length he took opportunity, by their disorderly coming, to make an assault, when **he issued forth** and put them all to flight, with slaughter of a great number of them.

This did suppress all the rebellions of the Gauls in those parts, and furthermore, he himself in person went there, in the midst of winter, wherever he heard they did rebel: for that there was come a new supply out of Italy of three whole legions, of the which, two of them Pompey lent him, and the other legion, he himself had **levied** in Gaul about the river of Po.

But in a while the seeds of war, which had long since been secretly sown and scattered by the most powerful men in those warlike nations, broke forth into the greatest and most dangerous war that was in those parts. For everywhere they levied multitudes of men, and great riches besides, to fortify their strongholds. Furthermore the country where they rose was very ill to come unto, and specially at that time being winter, when the rivers were frozen, the woods and forests covered with snow, the meadows drowned with floods, and the fields so deep of snow that no ways were to be found, neither the marshes nor rivers to be discerned, all was so overflown and drowned with water: all which troubles together were enough (as they thought) to keep Caesar from setting upon the rebels. Many tribes had revolted together, the chief of them being the **Arverni** and **Carnutini**; the general who had the supreme command in war was **Vercingetorix**, whose father the

Gauls before had put to death, because they thought he (the father) aspired to make himself king.

Vercingetorix having disposed his army in several bodies, and set officers over them, drew over to him all the country round about as far as those that lie upon the Arar; and having intelligence of the opposition which Caesar now experienced at Rome, thought to engage all Gaul in the war. So that if he had but tarried a little longer, until Caesar had entered into his civil wars, he would have put all Italy in as great fear and danger as it was when the Cimbri did come and invade it.

But Caesar, who above all men was gifted with the faculty of making the right use of everything in war, and most especially of seizing the right moment: so soon as he understood the news of the rebellion, he departed with speed, and returned back the selfsame way which he had gone, making the barbarous people know that they should deal with an army **invincible**, and which they could not possibly withstand, considering the great speed he had made with the same, in so sharp and hard a winter. For where they would not possibly have believed that a **post or courier** could have come in so short a time from the place where he was, unto them: they wondered when they saw him burning and destroying the country, the towns and strong forts where he came with his army, taking all to mercy that yielded unto him. Till at last the **Aedui**, who hitherto had styled themselves "brethren to the Romans," and had been much honoured by them, declared against him, and joined the rebels, to the great discouragement of his army.

Part Two

Accordingly he removed thence, and passed the **country of the Ligones**, desiring to reach the territories of the Sequani, who were his friends, and who lay like a bulwark in front of Italy against the other tribes of Gaul. There the enemy came upon him, and surrounded him with many **myriads**, whom he also was eager to engage; and at last, after some time and with much slaughter, he gained generally a complete victory; though at first he appears to have met with some reverse, and the Arverni will show you a small sword hanging up in a temple, which they say was taken from Caesar. Insomuch as Caesar himself coming that way by occasion, saw it, and fell a-laughing at it.

But some of his friends going about to take it away, he would not suffer them, but bade them let it alone, and touch it not, for it was a holy thing.

After the defeat, a great part of those who had escaped fled with their king into a town called **Alesia**, which Caesar besieged, though the height of the walls, and number of those who defended them, made it appear **impregnable**; and meantime, from without the walls, he was assailed by a greater danger than can be expressed. For the choice men of Gaul, picked out of each nation, and well-armed, came to relieve Alesia, to the number of three hundred thousand; nor were there in the town less than one hundred and seventy thousand.So that Caesar, being shut up betwixt two such forces, was compelled to protect himself by two walls, one towards the town, the other against the relieving army, as knowing if these forces should join, his affairs would be entirely ruined. For there, in that instant and extreme danger, he showed more valiantness and wisdom than he did in any battle he fought before.

But what a wonderful thing was this? that they of the city never heard anything of them that came to aid them, until Caesar had overcome them: and furthermore, that the Romans themselves which kept watch upon the wall that was built against the city, knew also no more of it than they, but when it was done, and that they heard the cries and lamentations of men and women in Alesia, when they perceived on the other side of the city such a number of glistering shields of gold and silver, such store of bloody armour, such a deal of **plate and moveables**, and such a number of tents and pavilions after the fashion of the Gauls, which the Romans had gotten of their spoils in their camp. So soon did so vast an army dissolve and vanish like a ghost or dream, the greatest part of them being killed upon the spot.

Furthermore, after they within the city of Alesia had done great hurt to Cæsar, and themselves also: in the end, they all yielded themselves. And Vercingetorix (he that was their king and captain in all this war) went out of the gates excellently well-armed, and his horse furnished with rich **caparison** accordingly, and rode round about Caesar, who sat in his chair of estate. Then lighting from his horse, he took off his **caparison and furniture**, and unarmed himself, and laid all on the ground, and went and sat down at Caesar's feet, and said never a word. So Caesar at length committed him as a prisoner taken in the wars, to lead him afterwards in his triumph at Rome.

Narration and Discussion

"For there, in that instant and extreme danger, he showed more valiantness and wisdom than he did in any battle he fought before." Explain.

Creative narration: You work at the Roman News Magazine (you can give it a better name), and your job is to design the cover. This month's feature is about Caesar's wars in the north. What will the headlines say? What illustration will you use? (You can use this narration activity in other lessons as well.)

Lesson Six

Introduction

The struggle for power in Rome was becoming ugly. Some wanted to bring back the authority of a king or a dictator, to end the chaos; or at least elect a powerful consul to do the same thing, and the obvious choice for that was Pompey. He was elected for a third term as consul in 52 B.C., the same year as Caesar's victory at Alesia.

Vocabulary

be beforehand: act before the other person did

apprehensions: worries

retired: retreated

bare suffrages: mere votes

monarchy: a state ruled by a king (or queen)

in Caesar's room: in the position of governor of Gaul

silver drachmas: coins

declare for him: declare him their new leader

presumptuous: overconfident

carried great semblance of reason: seemed quite reasonable

as private persons: out of office, without authority

tyrant: one who rules as a dictator, making decisions as he/she pleases. The Romans had a formal "dictatorship" that was used when the times required it, but that sort of dictator was seen as acting for the good of the state rather than in his own interests. "Tyranny" recalled the era of kings in Rome, prior to the Republic: so allowing one person as ruler, for more than a limited time, was something most Romans wanted to avoid at any cost.

lay down their commissions: give up their public positions

for the execution of his enterprise: to do what he intended

posterity: descendants

stayed: paused

People

Antony: Mark Antony (see introductory notes)

Scipio: Quintus Caecilius Metellus Pius Scipio Nasica; a senator, consul (52 B.C.), and military commander.

Lentulus: Lucius Cornelius Lentulus Crus, consul in 49 B.C., along with **Marcellus (Maior).** *Special note on the Marcellus family for anyone reading a version without omissions:* In 51 B.C., one of the consuls was Marcus Claudius Marcellus, often referred to simply as **Marcellus**; he was the brother of **Marcellus (Maior).** In 50 B.C., the two consuls were Lucius Aemilius Lepidus Paullus (or Paul the Consul) and Gaius Claudius Marcellus, called **Marcellus (Minor)**, a cousin of the other two. Referring to the time when "Marcellus" was consul can cause confusion, but it probably means 51 B.C.

Asinius Pollio: Gaius Asinius Pollio, a Roman orator and historian

Historic Occasions

50 B.C.: The Senate ordered Caesar to disband his army and return to Rome because his term as governor had ended

January, 49 B.C.: Caesar crossed the Rubicon into Italy, an act of defiance which began a civil war

On the Map

Ariminum: the modern city of Rimini, in northern Italy

river of Rubicon: see previous lesson

Reading

Part One

Caesar had long ago resolved upon the overthrow of Pompey, as had Pompey, for that matter, upon his. For Crassus, the fear of whom had hitherto kept them in peace, had been killed in Parthia; so that if the one of them wished to make himself the greatest man in Rome, he had only to overthrow the other; and if he again wished to prevent his own fall, he had nothing for it but to **be beforehand** with him whom he feared.

Pompey had not been long under any such **apprehensions**, having till lately despised Caesar, as thinking it no difficult matter to put down him whom he himself had advanced. But Caesar had entertained this design from the beginning against his rivals, and had **retired**, like an expert wrestler, to prepare himself apart for the combat. Making the Gallic wars his exercise-ground, he had at once improved the strength of his soldiery, and had heightened his own glory by his great actions, so that he was looked on as one who might challenge comparison with Pompey.

Nor did he let go any of those advantages which were now given him both by Pompey himself and the times, and the ill-government of Rome, where all who were candidates for offices publicly gave money, and without any shame bribed the people, who, having received their pay, did not contend for their benefactors with their **bare suffrages**, but with bows, swords, and slings. So that after having many times stained the place of election with blood of men killed upon the spot, they left the city at last without a government at all, to be carried about like a ship without a pilot to steer her; while all who had any wisdom could only be thankful if a course of such wild and stormy disorder and madness might end no worse than in a **monarchy**.

[Omission for length: Many people thought that giving Pompey sole power would be their only chance to restore order in Rome. This did not happen, but Pompey continued to have a great deal of power in the Senate, and also commanded a sort of private army (said to be bodyguards). Caesar, for his part, began to make large gifts to influential people who might support his cause. In 50 B.C., he sent a request to Rome that his term as governor of Gaul should be extended; but the Senate ordered him to disband his army and return to Rome as a private citizen.]

Part Two

> Furthermore, it was found that a captain or
> centurion sent from Caesar, being near unto the
> Senate, understanding that the council would not
> prolong Caesar's government which he required,
> clapping his hand upon the handle of his sword:
> "Well," said he, "this shall give it him." (Plutarch's
> *Life of Pompey*)

Pompey, alarmed at Caesar's attempts to buy people's favour, now openly took steps, both by himself and his friends, to have a successor appointed **in Caesar's room**, and sent to demand back the soldiers whom he had lent him to carry on the wars in Gaul. Caesar returned them, and made each soldier a present of two hundred and fifty **drachmas**. The officer who brought them home to Pompey spread amongst the people no very fair or favourable report of Caesar, and flattered Pompey himself with false suggestions that he was wished for by Caesar's army; and though his affairs here in some embarrassment through the envy of some, and the ill state of the government, yet there the army was at his command; and if they once crossed into Italy they would presently **declare for him**, so weary were they of Caesar's endless expeditions, and so suspicious of his designs for a monarchy.

Upon this Pompey grew **presumptuous**, and neglected all warlike preparations, as fearing no danger; and he used no other means against him than mere speeches and votes, for which Caesar cared nothing *[omission]*. Notwithstanding, the requests that Caesar propounded **carried great semblance of reason** with them. For he said that he was contented to lay down arms, so that Pompey did the like; and that both of them **as private persons** should come and make suit of their citizens to obtain honourable recompense: declaring that in taking arms from him, and granting them unto Pompey, they did wrongfully accuse him in going about to make himself a **tyrant**, and in the meantime to grant the other man the means to be a tyrant *[omission]*.

Then **Antony**, one of the tribunes, brought a letter sent from Caesar, and made it openly to be read in despite of the consuls. But **Scipio** in the Senate, Pompey's father-in-law, made this motion: that if Caesar did not dismiss his army by a certain day appointed him, the Romans should proclaim him an enemy unto Rome. And the consuls, putting it to the question whether Pompey should dismiss his soldiers, and again, whether Caesar should disband his, very few assented to the first, but almost all to the latter. But Antony proposing again that both should **lay down their commissions**, all but a very few agreed to it. Scipio was upon this very violent, and **Lentulus** the consul cried aloud that they had need of arms, and not of suffrages, against a robber; so that the senators for the present adjourned, and appeared in mourning as a mark of their grief for the dissension. After that, there came other letters from Caesar, which seemed much more reasonable: in the which he requested that they would grant him the nearer part of Gaul, and Illyria, with two legions only, and then that he would request nothing else, until he made suit for the consulship.

Part Three

Now at that time, Caesar had not in all about him above five thousand footmen, and three thousand horsemen: for the rest of his army, he left on the other side of the mountains, to be brought after him by his lieutenants. So, considering that **for the execution of his enterprise**, he should not need so many men of war at the first, but rather suddenly stealing upon them, so to astound his enemies with the boldness of it, taking benefit of the opportunity of time: as it would be easier, he thought, to throw them into consternation by doing what they never anticipated than fairly to conquer them, if he had alarmed them by his preparations.

And therefore he commanded his captains and lieutenants to go before, without any other armour than their swords, to take the city of **Ariminum** (a great city of Gaul, being the first city men come to, when they come out of Gaul), with as little bloodshed and tumult, as they could possibly. He committed the care of these forces to Hortensius, and himself spent the day in public as a stander-by and spectator of the gladiators, who exercised before him.

A little before night he went into his lodging, and bathing his body a little, came afterwards into the hall amongst them, and made merry with them awhile, whom he had bidden to supper. Then when it was well forward night, and very dark, he rose from the table, and prayed his company to be merry, and no man to stir, for he would straight come to them again: howbeit he had secretly before commanded a few of his trustiest friends to follow him, not altogether, but some one way, and some another way. He himself in the meantime took a coach he had hired, and made as though he would have gone some other way at the first, but suddenly he turned back again towards the city of Ariminum.

When he was come unto the little **river of Rubicon**, which divideth Gaul on this side the Alps from Italy: he stayed upon a sudden. For, the nearer he came to execute his purpose, the more remorse he had in his conscience, to think what an enterprise he took in hand: and his thoughts also fell out more doubtful, when he entered into consideration of the desperateness of his attempt. So he fell into many thoughts with himself, and spoke never a word, wavering sometime one way, sometime another way [Dryden: *while he revolved with himself*], and often times changed his determination, contrary to himself. So did he talk much also with his friends he had with him, amongst whom was **Asinius Pollio**, telling them what mischiefs the beginning of this passage over that river would breed in the world, and how much their **posterity** and them that lived after them, would speak of it in time to come. But at length, casting from him with a noble courage all those perilous thoughts to come, and speaking these words which valiant men commonly say, that attempt dangerous and desperate enterprises,

"A desperate man feareth no danger, come on" [Dryden: *"The die is cast", which can also be translated "Let the die be cast"*]: he passed over the river, and when he was come over, he ran with his coach and never **stayed**, so that before daylight he was within the city of Ariminum, and took it.

[short omission for mature content]

Narration and Discussion

"Pompey had not been long under any such apprehensions, having till lately despised Caesar, as thinking it no difficult matter to put down him whom he himself had advanced." How was he mistaken?

Caesar said "that he was contented to lay down arms, so that Pompey did the like." If Pompey had (unexpectedly) agreed, do you think Caesar would have stuck to his word?

"To cross the Rubicon" is an expression we use to mean "the point of no return." What did it mean for Julius Caesar?

Creative narration #1: Plutarch says that when Caesar came to the Rubicon, "he fell into many thoughts with himself." You are Caesar: make a numbered list of your thoughts.

Creative narration #2: "The officer…spread amongst the people no very fair or favourable report of Caesar." How might he have carried out this discrediting campaign?

Lesson Seven

Introduction

The reaction to Caesar's taking of the city of Ariminum was immediate and violent. Hordes of people from outside Rome arrived in the city, hoping for protection in case of military attacks. Some people blamed Pompey for not co-operating more fully with Caesar; others blamed him for not controlling him. Both of the consuls fled from the city, along with many senators.

Vocabulary

succour: help, aid

deluge: flood

conflux: confluence; merging

tempestuous agitation: the city was in an uproar

in a state of anarchy: without government

tumult: confusion

deference: respect

plausibly: reasonably

pulpit or **pulpit for orations:** the Rostra, or speakers' platform

smiths: metalworkers, locksmiths

treat of peace: to discuss peace terms

created dictator…: see the definition of **tyrant** in **Lesson Six**

whose fathers before had been slain in Sulla's time: Remember that Julius Caesar was related to Sulla's enemy Marius, so this action was important to him personally.

People

Domitius (#1): Lucius Domitius Ahenobarbus, also referred to as Ahenobarbus. An enemy of Caesar, and the brother-in-law of Cato, he was praetor in 58 B.C., ran unsuccessfully for the consulship of 55 B.C. (defeated by Pompey and Crassus); was consul in 54 B.C.; and succeeded Caesar as governor of Gaul. He commanded the right wing of Pompey's army in the Battle of Pharsalus, and was killed afterwards while trying to escape from the captured city. Not to be confused with **Gnaeus Domitius Calvinus (#2)**, a general and

43

consul (53 B.C., 40 B.C.) who was loyal to Caesar and commanded the center of the army in the same battle.

Publius Servilius Isauricus: A friend of Caesar, and co-consul with him for 48 B.C.; son of the **Isauricus** who had been beaten out by Caesar for the office of *Pontifex Maximus.*

Historic Occasions

January 1, 49 B.C.: Gaius Claudius Marcellus and Lucius Cornelius Lentulus Crus took office as consuls

January 10, 49 B.C.: Caesar crossed the border of Cisalpine Gaul and Italy, which was a declaration of civil war.

January 12, 49 B.C.: Caesar captured Ariminum

January 17, 49 B.C.: The consuls left Rome (they went south to **Capua**)

June-August 49 B.C.: Caesar's victory over Pompey's supporters in Spain, and then his return to Rome

January 48 B.C.: Caesar began to move his troops out against Pompey

On the Map

Capua: a city in southern Italy, 16 miles (25 km) north of Naples

Corfinium: a fortified city on the eastern side of the Apennine Mountains

Dyrrhachium: or Dyrrachium; a city in what is now Albania. Pompey used Dyrrhachium as a storage site for supplies such as food; so Caesar hoped that if Pompey could be drawn away to fight elsewhere, his army might be cut off from those supplies.

Brundisium: This has several possible spellings: Brundisium, or Brundusium, or Brindisium, or (its present-day name) Brindisi; a city on the Adriatic Sea. North and Dryden spell it Brundusium, but **Brundisium** seems to be more currently accepted.

The Ionian Sea: the sea between Italy and Greece

Oricum: or Orikon; a Greek city in the northern part of **Epirus (now part of Albania).** The Roman province of **Epirus**, at this time, was part of the larger province of **Macedonia.**

Apollonia: a city of southern **Illyria** or **Illyricum. Illyricum** was located along the coast of the **Adriatic Sea**, north of the **River Drin**; south of the river was the province of **Macedonia.**

Reading

Part One

As soon as Ariminum was taken, wide gates, so to say, were thrown open, to let in war upon every land and sea alike; [and the laws were broken along with the state boundaries, *my paraphrase*]. Nor would one have thought that, as at other times, the mere men and women fled from one town of Italy to another in their consternation; but that the very towns themselves left their sites and fled for **succour** to each other. The city of Rome was overrun, as it were, with a **deluge**, by the **conflux** of people flying in from all the neighbouring places. Magistrates could no longer govern, nor the eloquence of any orator quiet it; it was all but suffering shipwreck by the violence of its own **tempestuous agitation** *[omission]*.

> Lentulus, being now entered into his consulship, along with Marcellus, did not assemble the Senate. But Cicero, lately returned out of Cilicia, tried to bring them to agreement, proposing that Caesar should leave Gaul, and all the rest of his army; reserving only two legions together with the government of Illyria; and should thus be put in nomination for a second consulship. Pompey liked not this motion, but Caesar's friends were contented to grant that he should have but one of his legions. But Lentulus still opposed it, and Cato cried out on the other side also, that Pompey did ill to be deceived again. So all treaty of peace was cut off.
> (Plutarch's *Life of Pompey*)

Pompey, sufficiently disturbed of himself, was yet more perplexed by the clamours of others; some telling him that he justly suffered for having armed Caesar against himself and the government; others blaming him for permitting Caesar to be insolently used by Lentulus, when he made such ample concessions, and offered such reasonable proposals towards an accommodation. Favonius bade him now stamp upon the ground; for once, talking big in the Senate, he desired them not to trouble themselves about making any preparations for the war, for that he himself, with one stamp of his foot, would fill all Italy with soldiers. Yet, still Pompey at that time had more forces than Caesar; but he was not permitted to pursue his own thoughts, but, being continually disturbed with false reports and alarms, as if the enemy was close upon him and carrying all before him, he gave way, and let himself be borne down by the general cry. He put forth an edict declaring the city to be **in a state of anarchy**, and left it, with orders that the Senate should follow him, and that no one should stay behind who did not prefer tyranny to their country and liberty.

The consuls at once fled, without making even the usual sacrifices; so did most of the servants, carrying off their own goods in as much haste as if they had been robbing their neighbours. There were some Romans also, that always loved Caesar, whose wits were then so troubled and beside themselves, with the fear they had conceived, that they also fled, and followed the stream of this **tumult**, without manifest cause or necessity. But above all things, it was a lamentable sight to see the city itself, that in this fear and trouble was left at all adventure, as a ship tossed in storm of sea, forsaken of her pilots, and despairing of her safety.

Their departure being thus miserable, yet men esteemed their own banishment (for the love they bore unto Pompey) to be their natural country, and reckoned Rome no better than Caesar's camp. At that time also Labienus, who was one of Caesar's greatest friends, and who had been always used as his lieutenant in the wars of Gaul, and had valiantly fought in his cause: he likewise forsook him then, and fled unto Pompey.

Part Two

Caesar sent all his money and equipage after him, and then sat down before **Corfinium**, which was garrisoned with thirty cohorts under the command of **Domitius (#1)**. Domitius, in despair of maintaining the defense, requested a physician, whom he had among his attendants, to give him poison; and taking the dose, drank it, thinking to have died. But soon after, when he was told that Caesar showed the utmost clemency towards those he took prisoners, he lamented his misfortune, and blamed the hastiness of his resolution. The physician did comfort him again, and told him, that he had taken a drink, only to make him sleep, but not to destroy him. Then Domitius rejoiced, and went straight and yielded himself unto Caesar, who gave him his life; but he notwithstanding stole away immediately, and fled unto Pompey.

When these news were brought to Rome, they did marvellously rejoice and comfort them that still remained there; and moreover there were some of them that had forsaken Rome, which returned thither again. Caesar took into his army Domitius's soldiers, as he did all those whom he found in any town enlisted for Pompey's service. Being now strong and formidable enough, he advanced against Pompey himself, who did not stay to receive him, but fled to **Brundisium**, having sent the consuls before with a body of troops to **Dyrrhachium**. Soon after, upon Caesar's approach, he set to sea (as shall be more particularly related in his *Life*). Caesar would have immediately pursued him, but needed ships, and therefore went back to Rome, having made himself master of all Italy without bloodshed in the space of sixty days.

Part Three

When he was come to Rome, and found it much quieter than he looked for, and many senators present, to whom he addressed himself with courtesy and **deference**, desiring them to send to Pompey about any reasonable accommodations towards a peace. But nobody complied with this proposal; whether out of fear of Pompey, whom they had deserted, or that they thought Caesar did not mean what he said, but only thought it in his interest to talk **plausibly**.

Afterwards, when Metellus, the tribune, would have hindered him from taking money out of the public treasury, and cited some laws against it, Caesar replied that arms and laws had their own time.

> "Tush," said he, "time of war and law are two things.
> If this that I do," quoth he, "do offend thee, then get
> thee hence for this time: for war cannot abide this

frank and bold speech. But when wars are done, and
that we are all quiet again, then thou shalt speak in
the **pulpit** what thou wilt: and yet I do tell thee this
of favour, impairing so much my right, for thou art
mine, both thou and all them that have risen against
me, and whom I have in my hands."

Having said this to Metellus, he went to the doors of the treasury, and,
the keys not to be found, sent for **smiths** to force them open. Metellus
again making resistance and some encouraging him in it, Caesar, in a
louder tone, told him he would put him to death if he gave him any
further disturbance.

"Young man," quoth he, "thou knowest it is harder for me to tell
it thee, than to do it." That word made Metellus quake for fear, that he
got him away roundly: and ever after that, Caesar had all at his
commandment for the wars.

*[Omission for length: Instead of attacking Pompey directly, Caesar first went to
Spain and captured Pompey's forces there for his own army.]*

Part Four

When Caesar returned again to Rome, Piso, his father-in-law, gave him
counsel to send ambassadors unto Pompey, to **treat of peace**. But
Isauricus, to flatter Caesar, was against it.

Caesar being then **created dictator** by the Senate, called home
again all the banished men, and restored their children to honour,
whose fathers before had been slain in Sulla's time: and he relieved
the debtors by an act remitting some part of the interest on their debts,
and besides, did make some such other ordinances as those, but very
few. For he was dictator but eleven days only, and then did yield it up
of himself, and having declared himself consul, with **Publius Servilius
Isauricus**, hastened again to the war.

He marched so fast that he left all his army behind him, and went
himself before with six hundred horse, and five legions only of
footmen, in the winter quarter, about the month of January *[omission]*.
Then having passed over the **Ionian Sea**, and landed his men, he won
the cities of **Oricum** and **Apollonia**. Then he sent his ships back again
unto Brundisium, to transport the rest of his soldiers that could not

come with that speed he did. They as they came by the way, (like men whose strength of body was decayed) being wearied with so many sundry battles as they had fought with their enemies, could not but exclaim against Caesar,

> "When at last, and where, will this Caesar let us be
> quiet? He carries us from place to place, and uses us
> as if we were not to be worn out, and had no sense
> of labour. Even our iron itself is spent by blows, and
> we ought to have some pity on our bucklers and
> breastplates, which have been used so long. Our
> wounds, if nothing else, should make him see that
> we are mortal men whom he commands, subject to
> the same pains and sufferings as other human
> beings. The very gods themselves cannot force the
> winter season, or hinder the storms in their time;
> yet he pushes forward, as if he were not pursuing,
> but flying from an enemy."

Still marching on, by small journeys, they came at length unto the city of Brundisium. But when they were come, and found that Caesar had already passed over the sea, then they straight changed their complaints and minds. For they blamed themselves, and took on also with their captains, because they had not made them make more haste in marching; and sitting upon the rocks and cliffs of the sea, they looked over the main sea, towards the realm of **Epirus**, to see if they could discern the ships returning back, to transport them over.

Narration and Discussion

How did Caesar make himself "master of all Italy without bloodshed in the space of sixty days?"

Why did the soldiers' discovery that Caesar had already arrived in Greece ahead of them "straight change their complaints and minds?"

"Time of war and law are two things." Do you agree?

Creative narration: This might be a good time to produce another cover for the Roman News Magazine (**Lesson Five**). Who or what should be on the cover? What is the top story? Are there any other special features in this issue, perhaps a contest or a pull-out poster?

Lesson Eight

Introduction

Julius Caesar and Mark Antony gathered an army together in Epirus to fight Pompey's resistance troops. They lost the Battle of Dyrrhachium, but not the war, because, according to Caesar, Pompey had victory in his hands but did not know what to do with it. Both armies then moved on to Thessaly, where a final showdown was in the air.

Vocabulary

tack about: to change a boat's course by sailing into the wind

discovered himself: revealed himself

pinnace: small boat

young gentlemen and Roman knights: the cavalry

devise some fetch: come up with a scheme

javelin: a light spear which is thrown

with an impetus: with force

the general concurrence: the rest of the fighting

apprehensive: fearful

blemish: scar

shifted him: hurried to do a job; got moving

People

Spinther: Publius Cornelius Lentulus, nicknamed Spinther

Gnaeus Domitius Calvinus (#2): see note in **Lesson Seven**.

Quintus Cornificius: quaestor for Illyricum in 48 B.C.

Calenus: Quintus Fufius Calenus, Roman general and consul (47 B.C.)

Historic Occasions

48 B.C.: Caesar was declared dictator, but resigned after eleven days and declared himself consul instead, along with **Isauricus**.

48 B.C.: Caesar renewed his pursuit of Pompey. (What had Pompey been doing all this time? Training his army, according to Plutarch: "… they were men of all sorts, and raw soldiers untrained, whom Pompey continually exercised, lying at the city of Beroea…")

July, 48 B.C.: Battle of Dyrrhachium

August 48 B.C.: Pompey's defeat at the Battle of Pharsalus

On the Map

Gomphi: a town of **Thessaly** which guarded two passes through the mountains.

country of Pharsalus: Pharsalus was a city of Thessaly. However, the battle was likely fought on the Pharsalian Plain, rather than very close to the city itself.

Scotussa: another town of Thessaly

Reading

Part One

He in the meantime was posted in Apollonia, but had not an army with him able to fight the enemy, the forces from Brundisium being so long in coming, which put him to great suspense and embarrassment what to do. At last, he resolved upon a most hazardous experiment, and embarked, without anyone's knowledge, in a boat of twelve oars, to cross over to Brundisium, though the sea was at that time covered with a vast fleet of the enemy. He got on board in the night-time, in the dress of a slave, and throwing himself down like a person of no consequence, lay along at the bottom of the vessel. The river Anius was to carry them down to sea, and there used to blow a gentle gale every morning from the land, which made it calm at the mouth of the river, by driving the waves forward; but this night there had blown a strong wind from the sea, which overpowered that form the land, so that where the river met the influx of the sea-water, and the opposition of the waves, it was extremely rough and angry; and the current was beaten back with such a violent swell that the master of the boat could not make good his passage, but ordered his sailors to **tack about** and return.

Caesar, hearing that, straight **discovered himself** unto the master of the **pinnace**, who at the first was amazed when he saw him: but Caesar then taking him by the hand said unto him, "Good fellow, be of good cheer, and forwards hardily, fear not, for thou hast Caesar and his fortune with thee." The mariners, when they heard that, forgot the storm, and laying all their strength to their oars, did what they could to force their way down the river. But when it was to no purpose, and the vessel now took in much water, Caesar finding himself in such danger in the very mouth of the river, much against his will permitted the master to turn back.

When he was come to land, his soldiers ran to him in a multitude, reproaching him for what he had done, and indignant that he should think himself not strong enough to get a victory by their sole assistance, but must disturb himself, and expose his life for those who were absent, as if he could not trust those who were with him.

Part Two

After this, Antony came over with the forces from Brundisium, which encouraged Caesar to give Pompey battle, though he (Pompey) was encamped very advantageously, and furnished with plenty of provisions, both by sea and land, whilst Caesar was at the beginning but ill supplied, and before the end was extremely pinched for want of necessaries, so that his soldiers were forced to dig up a kind of root which grew there, and tempering it with milk, to feed on it.

Furthermore, they did make bread of it also, and advancing up to the enemy's outposts, would throw these loaves at the guards, telling them, that as long as the earth produced such roots they would not give up blockading Pompey. But Pompey took what care he could that neither the loaves nor the words should reach his men, who were out of heart and despondent through terror at the fierceness and hardihood of their enemies, whom they looked upon as a sort of wild beasts.

[Omission for length: During several minor battles, Caesar's army seemed to be coming out ahead, except for one event, the **Battle of Dyrrhachium**, *where Pompey was, technically, victorious; he failed to follow through and take the camp, but it was a close call just the same. That incident shook the morale of Caesar's soldiers, and food supplies were running low (which caused an outbreak of disease in the camp). Caesar, frustrated and worried, raised his camp, intending to go and attack Scipio in Macedonia instead. Pompey's officers assumed that Caesar's troops were retreating, and wanted to pursue them. Pompey disagreed, predicting that the worn-out army would soon "fall of itself"; but he was eventually pressured into following them. Caesar's army had a sudden turn of fate after capturing the city of* **Gomphi** *in Thessaly: they now had plenty of food and wine, and they quickly recovered both their health and their motivation to fight.]*

Part Two

When they both came into the **country of Pharsalus**, and both camps lay before the other, Pompey returned again to his former determination to avoid fighting, partly because he had ill signs and tokens of misfortune in his sleep. But they that were about him grew to such boldness and security, assuring themselves of victory, that Domitius (#1), **Spinther**, and Scipio, as if they had already conquered, quarreled which should succeed Caesar as *Pontifex Maximus*. And many sent to Rome to take houses fit to accommodate consuls and praetors, as being sure of entering upon those offices as soon as the battle was over.

But besides those, the **young gentlemen and Roman knights** were marvellous desirous to fight, that were bravely mounted, and armed with glistering gilt armours, their horses fat and very finely kept, and themselves goodly young men, to the number of seven thousand; where the gentlemen of Caesar's side were but one thousand only. The number of his footmen also were much after the same reckoning; for he had five, and Pompey's forty thousand, against two and twenty thousand.

Wherefore Caesar called his soldiers together, and told them how **Quintus Cornificius** was at hand, who brought two whole legions, and that he had fifteen cohorts led by **Calenus**, the which he made to stay about Megara and Athens. Then he asked them if they would await that aid, or whether they would rather venture battle by themselves alone. The soldiers cried out to him, and prayed him not to defer battle, but rather to **devise some fetch** to make the enemy fight as soon as he could.

[Omission: Caesar sacrificed to the gods and asked for predictions of success; the soothsayer would only promise "a marvellous great change."]

Part Three

The night before the battle, as he went about midnight to visit the watch, there was a light seen in the heavens, very bright and flaming, which seemed to pass over Caesar's camp and fall into Pompey's. In the morning also, when they relieved the watch, they heard a false alarm in the enemies' camp, without any apparent cause: which they commonly call a sudden fear that makes men besides themselves. This notwithstanding, Caesar thought not to fight that day, but was determined to have raised his camp from thence, and to have gone towards the city of **Scotussa**: and his tents in his camp were already overthrown when his scouts came in with great speed, to bring him news that his enemies were preparing themselves to fight.

Then he was very glad, and after he had made his prayers unto the gods to help him that day, he set his men in battle array, and divided them into three squadrons: giving the middle battle unto Domitius Calvinus (#2), and the left wing unto Antony, and placed himself in the right wing, choosing his place to fight in the tenth legion. But seeing that against his forces his enemies had set all their horsemen: he was half afraid when he saw the great number of them, and so brave besides. Wherefore he privately made six cohorts to come from the rearward of his battle, whom he had laid as an ambush behind his right wing, having first appointed his soldiers what they should do, when the horsemen of the enemies came to give them charge.

On the other side, Pompey placed himself in the right wing of his battle, gave the left wing unto Domitius (#1), and the middle battle unto Scipio, his father-in-law. Now all Pompey's knights (as we have told you before) were placed in the left wing, of purpose to surround Caesar's right wing behind, and to give their hottest charge there, where the general of their enemies was: making their account, that there was no squadron of footmen how thick soever they were, that could receive the charge of so great a troop of horsemen, but that they must necessarily be broken and shattered all to pieces upon the onset of so immense a force of cavalry.

When they were ready on both sides to give the signal for battle, Pompey commanded his foot, who were in the front, to stand their ground, and without breaking their order, receive, quietly, the enemy's first attack, till they came within a **javelin's** cast. Caesar, in this respect, also, blames Pompey's generalship, as if he had not been aware how the first encounter, when made **with an impetus** and upon the run, gives weight and force to the strokes, and fires the men's spirits into a flame, which **the general concurrence** fans to full heat.

[omission for length]

Whilst the foot was thus sharply engaged in the main battle, on the flank Pompey's horse rode up confidently, and opened their ranks very wide, that they might surround the right wing of Caesar. But before they engaged, Caesar's cohorts rushed out and attacked them, and did not dart their javelins at a distance, nor strike at the thighs and legs, as they usually did in close battle, but aimed at their faces. For thus Caesar had instructed them, in hope that young gentlemen, who had not known much of battles and wounds, but came wearing their hair long, in the flower of their age and height of their beauty, would be more **apprehensive** of such blows, and not care for hazarding both a danger at present and a **blemish** for the future. And so it proved, for they were so far from bearing the stroke of the javelins, that they could not stand the sight of them, but turned about, and covered their faces to secure them.

Once in disorder, presently they turned about to fly; and so most shamefully ruined all. For those who had beat them back at once outflanked the infantry, and, falling on them at the rear, cut them to pieces. Pompey, seeing his horsemen from the other wing of his battle so scattered and dispersed, fleeing away, forgot that he was any more "Pompey the Great," but rather was like a man whose wits the gods had taken from him, being afraid and amazed with the slaughter sent from above; and so retired into his tent, speaking never a word, and sat there to see the end of this battle. Until at length all his army being overthrown, and put to flight, the enemies came, and got up upon the ramparts and defense of his camp, and fought hand to hand with them that stood to defend the same. Then as a man come to himself again, he spoke but this only: "What, even into our camp?" So in haste, casting off his coat of armour and apparel of a general, he **shifted him**, and put on such clothing, as became his miserable fortune, and so stole out of his camp. Furthermore, what he did after this overthrow, and how he had put himself into the hands of the Egyptians, by whom he was miserably slain: we have set it forth at large in his *Life*.

[omission for length]

Narration and Discussion

What were some of the good and not-so-good decisions that Caesar and Pompey made during the Battle of Pharsalus?

For older students and further thought: Was Caesar's command to "aim at their faces" justified?

Creative narration #1: "Caesar then taking him by the hand said unto him, 'Good fellow, be of good cheer, and forwards hardily, fear not, for thou hast Caesar and his fortune with thee.'" Tell the story from the captain's point of view.

Creative Narration #2: After the **Battle of Dyrrhachium**, Caesar moved most of his troops into the region of Thessaly (in Greece), and took the city of Gomphi. Another source says that at this time he reconnected with Domitius Calvinus (#2), during the time that his men were taking their "holiday." Imagine a conversation that might have taken place between a) Caesar and Domitius or b) some of the soldiers.

Lesson Nine

Introduction

Julius Caesar tracked Pompey to Egypt, but he was too late: Pompey had already been put to death there. At this point Caesar might have returned to Rome; but he became involved in Egyptian politics, and also with the Pharaoh's sister, Cleopatra. He also fought with Pharnaces, the king of Pontus.

Vocabulary

men of estimation: nobles or other respected citizens

eunuch: a type of royal servant who was often in charge of the women's quarters or who managed household affairs. This particular eunuch held an unusually influential position at the Egyptian court.

under pretense of arrears of debt: saying that it was owed to them as payment of an old debt

myriad: "Myriad" means ten thousand, and was often used to refer to numbers of soldiers; but it was also a unit of currency.

remitted: Caesar had forgiven or cancelled part of the debt

fardel: package, bundle

in fine: in short; to sum up

destroyed the great library of Alexandria: Other sources say that the fire did not much damage the library, and that it was destroyed later.

But as for the king…: King Ptolemy XIII is assumed to have drowned during the battle.

wrote three words…: the historian Suetonius says that they were inscribed on a tablet which was carried during Caesar's triumph.

People

Cleopatra: she became co-ruler with another brother, Ptolemy XIV

Pothinus the eunuch: or Potheinus; a high-ranking servant of King Ptolemy XIII, and also his regent since Ptolemy was very young

Achillas: a guardian of King Ptolemy; one of the murderers of Pompey

Caesarion: Caesar's son (it is assumed), and the last pharaoh of Egypt

Pharnaces: Pharnaces II of Pontus, whose father Mithridates VI had conquered a number of neighbouring territories (including **Bithynia** and **Cappadocia**), but who was defeated by the Romans himself

Historic Occasions

48 B.C.: Caesar followed Pompey to Egypt, but arrived after his death.

48/47 B.C.: Caesar's adventures in the Egyptian civil war

47 B.C.: the Battle of Zela, against Pharnaces II of Pontus

On the Map

Pharos: the famous lighthouse at Alexandria

Syria: a Middle Eastern country which had become a Roman province

Pontus: a region on the southern coast of the **Black Sea**

Lesser Armenia: the part of Armenia lying north and west of the **Euphrates River**

Zela: now called Zile, a city in Turkey

Reading

Part One

As for the foot soldiers of Pompey that were taken prisoners, Caesar did put many of them amongst his legions, and did pardon also many **men of estimation**; among whom Brutus was one, that afterwards slew Caesar himself; and it is reported that Caesar was very sorry for him when he could not immediately be found after the battle, and that he rejoiced again when he knew he was alive, and that he (Brutus) came to yield himself unto him.

[omission for length]

Caesar treated kindly all Pompey's friends and familiars who, wandering up and down the country, were taken of the king of Egypt; and won them all to be at his commandment. Continuing these courtesies, he wrote unto his friends at Rome that the greatest pleasure he took of his victory was that he daily saved the lives of some of his countrymen that bore arms against him.

As to the war in Egypt, some say it was at once dangerous and dishonourable, and no ways necessary, but occasioned only by his passion for **Cleopatra**. Others blame the ministers of the king, and especially the **eunuch** Pothinus, who was the chief favourite and who had lately killed Pompey; had banished Cleopatra, and was now secretly plotting Caesar's destruction (to prevent which, Caesar from that time began to sit up whole nights, under pretense of drinking, for the security of his person.) And, openly, Pothinus was intolerable in his affronts to Caesar, both by his words and actions. For when Caesar's soldiers had musty and unwholesome corn measured out to them, Pothinus told them they must be content with it, since they were fed at another's cost. He also ordered that his table should be served with wooden and earthen dishes, and said Caesar had carried off all the gold and silver plate, **under pretense of arrears of debt**. For the present king's father owed Caesar one thousand seven hundred and fifty **myriads** of money. Caesar had formerly **remitted** to his children the rest, but thought fit to demand the thousand myriads at that time to maintain his army. Pothinus told him that he had better go now and attend to his other affairs of greater consequence, and that he should receive his money at another time with thanks. Caesar replied that he did not want Egyptians to be his counsellors; and soon after he privately sent for Cleopatra from her retirement.

Part Two

She, taking only Apollodorus the Sicilian of all her friends, took a little boat, and went away with him in it in the night, and came and landed hard by the foot of the castle. Then having no other means to come into the court without being known, she laid herself down upon a mattress or flock bed, which Apollodorus her friend tied and bound up together like a bundle with a great leather thong, and so took her up on his back, and brought her thus hampered in this **fardel** unto Caesar, in at the castle gate. This was the first occasion, (as it is reported) that made Caesar to love her: but afterwards, when he saw her sweet conversation and pleasant entertainment, he fell then in further liking with her, and did reconcile her again unto her brother the king, with condition that they two jointly should reign together.

Part Three

Upon this new reconciliation, a great feast being prepared, a slave of Caesar's that was his barber, the fearfullest wretch that lived, still busily prying and listening abroad in every corner, being mistrustful by nature: found that Pothinus and **Achillas** did lie in wait to kill his master Caesar. This being proved unto Caesar, he did set such sure watch about the hall where the feast was made, that, **in fine**, he slew Pothinus himself. Achillas on the other side, saved himself, and fled unto the king's camp, where he raised a marvellous dangerous and difficult war for Caesar: because he having then but a few men about him as he had, he was to fight against a great and strong city.

The first danger he fell into was for the lack of water he had: for his enemies had stopped the mouth of the pipes which conveyed water unto the castle. The second danger he had was that, seeing his enemies came to take his ships from him, he was driven to repulse that danger with fire by setting fire to his own ships, which, after burning the docks, thence spread on and **destroyed the great library of Alexandria**. A third was when, in an engagement near **Pharos**, he leaped from into a small boat to assist his soldiers who were in danger, and when the Egyptians pressed him on every side, he threw himself into the sea, and with much difficulty swam off. It is said, that then holding divers books in his hand, he did never let them go, but kept them always upon his head above water, and swam with the other hand, notwithstanding that they shot marvellously at him, and was driven sometime to duck into the water; howbeit, the boat was drowned presently.

In fine, the king coming to his men that made war with Caesar, he went against him and gave him battle, and won it with great slaughter and effusion of blood. **But as for the king, no man could ever tell what became of him after**. Thereupon Caesar made **Cleopatra**, the king's sister, Queen of Egypt; who being great with child, was shortly brought to bed of a son, whom the Alexandrians named **Caesarion**.

From thence he went into **Syria**, and so going into Asia, there it was told him that Gnaeus Domitius Calvinus (#2) was overthrown in battle by **Pharnaces**, the son of King Mithridates, and was fled out of the realm of **Pontus** with a handful of men; and that Pharnaces was not contented with the winning of **Bithynia** and **Cappadocia**, but further would needs attempt to win **Lesser Armenia**, procuring all those kings, princes, and governors of the provinces thereabouts to rebel against the Romans. Thereupon Caesar went thither straight with three legions, and fought a great battle with King Pharnaces, by the city of **Zela**, where he slew his army, and drove him out of all the realm of Pontus. And because he would advertise one of his friends of the suddenness of this victory, he only **wrote three words unto his friend Amantius** at Rome: "Veni, Vidi, Vici": to wit, "I came, I saw, I overcame [*conquered*]." These three words ending all with like sound and letters in the Latin, have a certain short grace, more pleasant to the ear, than can be well expressed in any other tongue.

Hence he crossed into Italy, and came to Rome at the end of that year, for which he had been a second time chosen dictator [*omission*]; and was elected consul for the next.

Narration and Discussion

Caesar wrote that "the greatest pleasure he took of his victory was that he daily saved the lives of some of his countrymen that bore arms against him." Is this laudable or reasonable, considering that he had only recently been throwing spears at them?

Caesar's love affair with Cleopatra has been explored by many artists and storytellers. Do you find the story romantic, or head-shaking?

Creative narration #1: If you have not yet designed a cover for the Roman News Magazine (or if you would just like to do it again), create a special "Came, Saw, Conquered" edition.

Creative narration #2: If you could save a few books by swimming away with them (like Caesar), which ones would you take?

Lesson Ten

Introduction

Part One covers an important battle in what is now Tunisia. After Pompey's assassination in Egypt, his allies (the Optimates) had escaped to Roman territory in Africa, and had organized a resistance there. The force was led by Scipio and Marcus Cato the Younger, but involved others such as the two sons of Pompey, and King Juba of Numidia. Caesar and his troops landed in Africa in December of 47 B.C., and the **Battle of Thapsus**—a siege of the resistance army's stronghold there—took place a few months afterwards.

In Part Two, we have a brief description of the last battle of Caesar's civil war: the **Battle of Munda** against the sons of Pompey.

Vocabulary

> **engage:** make war against
>
> **the time of the winter solstice:** in December
>
> **in raillery:** in mockery; as a joke
>
> **peep:** put one's nose out of the camp (peek out); venture out
>
> **pell-mell:** hastily, and/or in a confused and disorderly manner
>
> **told him:** it's not clear whether Caesar was talking to the eagle or to the ensign bearer

carried: captured

reposed himself: rested

three triumphs: other sources say four, if the Gallic Wars are included

meet: proper

perpetual dictator: a permanent position of absolute power in Rome

deposed: removed from power

People

Scipio: Scipio Nasica (see note in **Lesson Five**)

King Juba I: king of Numidia from 60-46 B.C. After fleeing from certain defeat at the **Battle of Pharsalus**, it is believed that he and the Roman general Marcus Petreius formed a suicide pact, one of them killing the other and then ending his own life.

Gaius Asinius Pollio: a soldier, politician, historian, and writer

Afranius: former consul and Pompey's lieutenant in Spain

as it was professed: as it was officially stated

whose little son: Juba II, who became king of Numidia and Mauretania, and who was a respected scholar and author of books such as *Roman Archaeology*. He was raised in Rome by Julius Caesar and then by his nephew Octavian (Caesar Augustus).

Historic Occasions

46 B.C.: The year with three extra months, because of Caesar's change to the calendar. Julius Caesar was consul along with Marcus Aemilius Lepidus.

January, 46 B.C.: Caesar defeated by his former lieutenant Titus Labienus at the Battle of Ruspina

April, 46 B.C.: Caesar's victory at the Battle of Thapsus (and the deaths of Cato and Scipio by suicide)

April, 46 B.C.: Caesar's triple (or quadruple) triumph, celebrating his victories in Gaul, in Egypt, against Pharnaces, and against King Juba. Caesar was made dictator for ten years.

45 B.C.: Caesar was consul without a colleague (which was unusual).

March, 45 B.C.: Battle of Munda, in southern Spain (death of Titus Labienus)

April, 45 B.C.: Great celebrations were held to celebrate this final victory and the end of the civil war, but some found that offensive.

October 45 B.C.: Caesar resigned as sole consul, which allowed two consuls to be elected for the next year. He was re-elected consul for 44 B.C., along with Mark Antony.

January/February 44 B.C.: Caesar was declared perpetual dictator

On the Map

Africa: the Roman province called Africa, which included present-day Tunisia and parts of Algeria and Libya

Sicily: the very large island at the toe of Italy's "boot"

Numidia (Numidians): a kingdom of northwest Africa

Thapsus: a port city on Tunisia's Mediterranean coast

Reading

Part One

After the Battle of Pharsalus, Cato and **Scipio** fled into **Africa**, and there, with the assistance of **King Juba**, got together a considerable force, which Caesar resolved to **engage**. He accordingly passed into **Sicily** at about **the time of the winter solstice**, and to remove from his officers' minds all hopes of delay there, encamped by the seashore; and as soon as ever he had a fair wind, put to sea with three thousand foot and a few horse. When he had landed them, he went back secretly, under some apprehensions for the larger part of his army, but met them upon the sea, and brought them all to the same camp.

There he was informed that the enemies relied much upon an ancient oracle, that the house of the Scipios should be always victorious in Africa. There was in his army a man, otherwise mean and contemptible, but of that family, and his name was Cornelius Scipio Salvito. This man, Caesar (whether **in raillery** to ridicule Scipio, who commanded the enemy, or seriously to bring over the omen to his side, it were hard to say), put at the head of his troops, as if he were general, in all the frequent battles which he was compelled to fight.

For he was in such want both of victualling for his men, and forage for his horses, that he was forced to feed the horses with seaweed, which he washed thoroughly to take off its saltiness, and mixed with a little grass to give it a more agreeable taste. The **Numidians** (which are light horsemen, and very ready of service) being a great number together, would be on a sudden in every place, and spread all the fields over thereabout, so that no man dared **peep** out of the camp to go for forage. And one day as the men-of-arms were staying to behold an African doing notable things in dancing, and playing with the flute: they being set down quietly to take their pleasure of the view thereof, having in the meantime given their slaves their horses to hold, the enemies stealing suddenly upon them, compassed them in round about, and slew a number of them in the field, and, chasing the others also that fled, followed them **pell-mell** into their camp. Furthermore, had not Caesar himself, and **Gaius Asinius Pollio** with him, gone out of the camp to the rescue, and stayed them that fled, the war that day would have been ended.

There was also another skirmish where his enemies had the upper hand, in the which it is reported, that Caesar taking the ensign bearer by the collar that carried the Eagle in his hand, stayed him by force, and turning his face, **told him**: "See, there be thy enemies."

Scipio, flushed with this success at first, had a mind to come to one decisive action. He therefore left **Afranius** and Juba in two distinct bodies not far distant; and marched himself toward **Thapsus**, where he proceeded to build a fortified camp above a lake, to serve as a center-point for their operations, and also as a place of refuge.

Whilst Scipio was thus employed, Caesar, with incredible dispatch, made his way through thick woods and a country supposed to be impassable, cut off one part of the enemy and attacked another in the front. Having routed these, he followed up his opportunity and the current of his good fortune, and on the first onset **carried** Afranius's camp, and ravaged that of the Numidians (Juba, their king, being glad to save himself by flight); so that in a small part of a single day he made himself master of three camps, and killed fifty thousand of the enemy, with the loss only of fifty of his own men. This is the account some give of that fight.

Yet others do write also, that Caesar himself was not there in person at the execution of this battle. For as he did set his men in battle array, the falling sickness took him. He perceived the approaches of it, and before it had too far disordered his senses, when he was already beginning to shake under its influence, withdrew into a neighbouring fort where he **reposed himself**. Of the men of consular and praetorian dignity that were taken after the fight, several Caesar put to death; others [such as Cato] anticipated him by killing themselves.

[omission for length: the death of Cato]

Part Two

Caesar, upon his return to Rome, did not omit to pronounce before the people a magnificent account of his victory, telling them that he had subdued a country which would supply the public every year with two hundred thousand attic bushels of corn, and three million pounds' weight of oil. He then led **three triumphs** for Egypt, Pontus, and Africa: the last for the victory over, not Scipio, but King Juba, **as it was professed**, **whose little son** was then carried in the triumph, the happiest captive that ever was (and who *[omission]* came by this means to obtain a place among the most learned historians of Greece).

After the triumphs, he distributed rewards to his soldiers, and treated the people with feasting and shows. He entertained the whole people together at one feast, where twenty-two thousand dining couches were laid out; and he made a display of gladiators, and of battles by sea, in honour, as he said, of his daughter Julia, though she had been long since dead. When these shows were over, an account was taken of the people who, from three hundred and twenty thousand, were now reduced to one hundred and fifty thousand. So great a waste had the civil war made in Rome alone, not to mention what the other parts of Italy and the provinces suffered.

Part Three

After all these things were ended, Caesar was chosen consul the fourth time, and went into Spain to make war with the sons of Pompey, who were yet but very young, but had notwithstanding raised a marvellous great army together, and showed themselves to have had manhood and courage worthy to command such an army, insomuch as they put Caesar himself in great danger of his life.

*[Omission for length: details of Caesar's victory at the **Battle of Munda**.]*

But the triumph he made into Rome for the same, did as much offend the Romans, and more, than anything that ever he had done before: because he had not overcome captains that were strangers, nor barbarous kings, but had destroyed the sons of the noblest man in Rome, whom fortune had overthrown. And because he had plucked up his race by the roots, men did not think it **meet** for him to triumph so, for the calamities of his country, rejoicing at a thing for the which he had but one excuse to allege in his defense, unto the gods and men: that he was compelled to do that which he did. And the rather they thought it not meet, because he had never before sent letters nor messengers unto the commonwealth at Rome for any victory that he had ever won in all the civil wars: but did always for shame refuse the glory of it.

This notwithstanding, the Romans inclining to Caesar's prosperity, and taking the bit in the mouth, supposing that to be ruled by one man alone, it would be a good means for them to take breath a little, after so many troubles and miseries as they had abidden in these civil wars: they chose him **perpetual dictator**. This was a plain tyranny: for to this absolute power of dictator, they added this: never to be afraid to be **deposed**. Cicero propounded before the Senate that they should give him such honours as were meet for a man; howbeit, others afterwards added honours beyond all reason. For men striving who should most honour him, they made him hateful and troublesome to themselves that most favoured him, by reason of the unmeasurable greatness and honours which they gave him. His enemies, too, are thought to have had some share in this, as well as his flatterers. It gave them advantage against him, and would be their justification for any attempt they should make upon him; for since the civil wars were ended, he had nothing else that he could be charged with.

And they had good reason to decree a temple to Clementia, in token of their thanks for the mild use he made of his victory. For he not only pardoned many of those who fought against him, but, further, to some gave honours and offices; as particularly to Brutus and Cassius, who both of them were praetors.

And where Pompey's images had been thrown down, he caused them to be set up again: whereupon Cicero said then, that in Caesar setting up Pompey's images again, he made his own to stand the surer. And when some of his friends did counsel him to have a guard for the safety of his person, and some also did offer themselves to serve him: he would never consent to it, but said it was better to die once, than always to be afraid of death.

Narration and Discussion

"…they made him hateful and troublesome…by reason of the unmeasurable greatness and honours which they gave him." Is it possible to make someone an enemy by honouring him too much?

For further thought: Compare these statements: "And they had good reason to decree a temple to Clementia, in token of their thanks for the mild use he made of his victory." "So great a waste had the civil war made in Rome alone, not to mention what the other parts of Italy and the provinces suffered." Can both be true?

Creative narration #1: Write an account of the triumph from the point of view of Juba II (perhaps as a reminiscence in later years).

Creative narration #2: If you have not already been reading Shakespeare's play *Julius Caesar*, you may want to read or watch it now.

Shakespeare Connections

Shakespeare's play opens on the day of Caesar's triumph after his victory over the sons of Pompey. "Knew you not Pompey?" demands the tribune Marullus. "And do you now cull out a holiday? / And do you now strew flowers in his way, / That comes in triumph over Pompey's blood?" Shakespeare combines this event with the Feast of Lupercal (in **Lesson Eleven**), at which Caesar is publicly offered, but refuses, a crown. The Lupercal was held in February, but the triumph had actually taken place in October.

Lesson Eleven

Introduction

Now is a good time to review the things that Julius Caesar did over his long career, to see how things stood at the end of 45 B.C. Who were his friends? How did the people of Rome feel about him? Now that the wars were over, what did he want or expect?

Vocabulary

no place to repair unto: no home

preferments: appointments to high positions

a sort of emulous struggle with himself: Caesar was almost jealous of himself

honest colour: good reason

tearing open his doublet collar: pulling back his toga to expose his neck

affront: insult

diadem: a jeweled crown or headband

proof: test

named for the consulship four years after: This seems to have been a promise that Caesar made to Brutus, but it never took place.

the praetor's seat where he gave audience: the place where he carried out his duties and heard people's cases

seditious: rebellious

egg him on: encourage, provoke

jealousy: mistrust

carrion: dead, decaying flesh

People

Brutus, who had in old time…; the first Brutus: the ancestor of this Brutus; see Plutarch's *Life of Publicola*

Historic Occasions

44 B.C.: Julius Caesar and Mark Antony were consuls

44 B.C.: Marcus Brutus was praetor in Rome

Reading

Part One

But to win himself the love and goodwill of the people, as the honourablest guard and best safety he could have, Caesar made common feasts again, and general distributions of corn. Furthermore, to gratify the soldiers also, he replenished many cities again with inhabitants, which before had been destroyed, and placed them there that had **no place to repair unto**: of the which the noblest and chiefest cities were these two, Carthage, and Corinth *[omission]*.

And as for the men of high rank, he won them also, promising some of them to make them praetors and consuls in time to come; and unto others, offices and honours; but to all men generally good hope, seeking all the ways he could to make every man contented with his reign *[omission]*.

Caesar was born to do great things, and had a passion after honour;

and the many noble exploits he had done did not now serve as an inducement to him to sit still and reap the fruit of his past labours, but were incentives and encouragements to go on, and raised in him ideas of still greater actions, and a desire of new glory, as if the present were all spent. It was in fact **a sort of emulous struggle with himself**, as if it had been with another, how he might outdo his past actions by his future.

[Omission for length: Caesar had many plans and ideas, some of which were carried out and some not. One idea that he did put into action was the reworking of the calendar.]

Part Two

But the chiefest cause that made him mortally hated was the covetous desire he had to be called king: which first gave the people just cause, and next his secret enemies **honest colour** to bear him ill-will. This notwithstanding, they that procured him this honour and dignity gave it out among the people that it was written in the prophecies, how the Romans might overcome the Parthians if they made war with them, and were led by a king; but otherwise that they were unconquerable. And furthermore, they were so bold besides, that, Caesar returning to Rome from the city of Alba, when they came to salute him, they called him king. But the people being offended, and Caesar also angry, he said he was not called king, but Caesar. Then every man keeping silence, he went his way heavy and sorrowful.

When they had decreed divers honours for him in the Senate, the consuls and praetors, accompanied with the whole assembly of the Senate, went unto him in the marketplace, where he was set by the pulpit for orations, to tell him what honours they had decreed for him in his absence. But he, sitting still in his majesty, disdaining to rise up unto them when they came in, as if they had been private men, answered them that his honours had more need to be cut off, than enlarged. This treatment offended not only the Senate, but the commonalty too, as if they thought the affront upon the Senate equally reflected upon the whole Republic; so that all who could decently leave him went off, looking much discomposed.

Thereupon also Caesar rising, departed home to his house, and

tearing open his doublet collar, making his neck bare, he cried out aloud to his friends that his throat was ready to offer to any man that would come and cut it. But afterwards he made the malady from which he suffered the excuse for his sitting, saying that those who are attacked by it lose their presence of mind if they talk much standing; that they presently grow giddy, fall into convulsions, and quite lose their reason. But this was not the reality, for he would willingly have stood up to the Senate, had not Cornelius Balbus, one of his friends, or rather flatterers, hindered him. "Will you not remember," said he, "you are Caesar, and will you not let them reverence you, and do their duties?"

Part Three

[The Feast of Lupercal was a religious festival that included a foot race through the streets.]

He gave a fresh occasion of resentment by his **affront** to the tribunes at the Lupercalia *[omission]*. Caesar sat to behold that sport upon the pulpit for orations, in a chair of gold, appareled in triumphing manner. Antony, who was consul at that time, was one of them that ran this holy course. So when he came into the marketplace, the people made a lane for him to run at liberty, and he came to Caesar, and presented him a **diadem** wreathed about with laurel. Whereupon there rose a certain cry of rejoicing, not very great, done only by a few, appointed for the purpose. But when Caesar refused the diadem, then all the people together made an outcry of joy. Then Antony offering it him again, there was a second shout of joy, but yet of a few. But when Caesar refused it again the second time, then all the whole people shouted. Caesar having made this **proof**, found that the people did not like of it, and thereupon rose out of his chair, and commanded the crown to be carried unto Jupiter in the Capitol.

After that, there were set up images of Caesar in the city with diadems upon their heads, like kings. Those, the two tribunes, Flavius and Marullus, went and pulled down; and furthermore, meeting with them that first saluted Caesar as king, they committed them to prison. The people followed them rejoicing at it, and called them *Brutes*: because of **Brutus, who had in old time driven the kings out of Rome**, and that brought the kingdom of one person unto the government of the Senate and people. Caesar was so offended withal, that he deprived Marullus and Flavius of their tribuneships, and accusing them, he spoke also against the people, and called them *Bruti* and *Cumani*, to wit, beasts and fools.

Hereupon the people went straight unto Marcus Brutus, who from his father came of the first Brutus, and by his mother, of the Servilii, a noble house as any was in Rome, being besides nephew and son-in-law to Cato. Notwithstanding, the great honours and favour Caesar showed unto him took off the edge from the desires he might himself have felt for overthrowing the new monarchy. For Caesar did not only save his life, after the Battle of Pharsalus when Pompey fled, and did at his request also save many more of his friends besides: but furthermore, he put a marvellous confidence in him.

He had at that time the most honourable praetorship for the year, and was **named for the consulship four years after**, being preferred before Cassius, his competitor. Upon the question as to the choice, Caesar, it is related, said that Cassius had the fairer pretensions, but that he could not pass by Brutus. Some people one day accusing Brutus of practising this conspiracy, Caesar would not hear of it, but clapping his hand on his body, told them, "Brutus will look for this skin": meaning thereby, that Brutus for his virtue, deserved to rule after him; but yet, that for ambition's sake, he would not show himself unthankful nor dishonourable.

Now they that desired change, and wished Brutus only their prince and governor above all others: they dared not come to him themselves to tell him what they would have him to do, but in the night did cast sundry papers into **the praetor's seat where he gave audience**, most of them to this effect: "Thou sleepest, Brutus, and art not Brutus indeed." Cassius finding Brutus' ambition stirred up the more by these **seditious** bills, did prick him forward, and **egg him on** the more, for a private quarrel he had conceived against Caesar: the circumstance whereof, we have set down more at large in Brutus' *Life*.

Caesar also had Cassius in great **jealousy**, and suspected him much: whereupon he said on a time to his friends, "What will Cassius do, think ye? I like not his pale looks." Another time when Caesar's friends complained unto him of Antony, and Dolabella, that they pretended some mischief towards him: he answered them again, "As for those fat men and smooth-combed heads," quoth he, "I never reckon of them;

but these pale-visaged and **carrion**-lean people, I fear them most," meaning Brutus and Cassius.

Narration and Discussion

Did Caesar want to be a king? Was he already a king in everything but name?

Why did Caesar say that he distrusted pale, thin people?

Creative narration #1: Illustrate something from this lesson, using any art media you prefer.

Creative narration #2: Read or watch these scenes from Shakespeare's play.

Creative narration #3 (this one is a challenge): Long ago, Caesar had wept over the stories of Alexander's exploits, feeling that he himself had accomplished so little. Now (Plutarch says) he seemed to be almost jealous of his own success. Imagine a conversation between Caesar-now and Caesar-the-hero, discussing the problem.

Shakespeare Connections

"After that, there were set up images of Caesar in the city with diadems upon their heads, like kings. Those, the two tribunes, Flavius and Marullus, went and pulled down: and furthermore, meeting with them that first saluted Caesar as king, they committed them to prison." Shakespeare uses this (and the tribunes) in Act I Scene I, where Flavius says, "Disrobe the images, / If you do find them deck'd with ceremonies...let no images / Be hung with Caesar's trophies." In Scene II, Casca mentions that the tribunes have been "put to silence" for doing so.

In Act I Scene II, Caesar tells Calpurnia to stand directly in Antony' way when he runs past, and he tells Antony to make sure he touches Calpurnia. The Lupercal was a fertility festival, and to touch one of the runners might help her bear a son and heir for Caesar.

Antony says, "When Caesar says, 'Do this,' it is perform'd." When Caesar reformed the calendar, although it was an improvement to the former system, some people thought it was an additional example of his arrogance. Plutarch quoted Cicero, who once said that if Caesar said, "Tomorrow the star Lyra will rise," the response should be "'Yea, at the commandment of Caesar,' as if men were compelled so to say and think, by Caesar's edict."

"Cassius finding Brutus' ambition stirred up the more by these seditious bills, did prick him forward, and egg him on the more, for a private quarrel he had conceived against Caesar." In Act I Scene II, Shakespeare brings this scene to life. In Act II Scene I, Brutus says, "Since Cassius first did whet me against Caesar, / I have not slept."

"As for those fat men and smooth combed heads," quoth he, "I never reckon of them; but these pale-visaged and carrion-lean people, I fear them most," meaning Brutus and Cassius. In Act I Scene II, Shakespeare writes "Let me have men about me that are fat, / Sleek-headed men and such as sleep a-nights. / Yond Cassius has a lean and hungry look, / He thinks too much; such men are dangerous."

During the Lupercal, Brutus hears shouting but doesn't see what happened. Afterwards he asks Casca for his narration of the events. "I saw Mark Antony offer him a crown—yet 'twas not a crown neither, 'twas one of these coronets..." Shakespeare adds a bit more drama to the scene by saying that Caesar then "fell down in the market-place, and foam'd at mouth, and was speechless"; and that (according to Casca) "he pluck'd me ope his doublet; and offer'd them his throat to cut." This is something that Plutarch describes just before the scene at the Lupercal.

Lesson Twelve

Introduction

As you read this last passage, watch for differences between what you may have seen or read in other sources, and what Plutarch actually said (for instance, about Caesar's last words).

Not you too?

Shakespeare's Julius Caesar says "Et tu, Brute?" to Brutus, and those words are quoted today as an accusation to a traitorous friend. The historian Suetonius said that the remark was something like "You too, son?" But Plutarch said that when Caesar died, he had pulled his toga over his head, so nobody knows what his last words were.

Vocabulary

contending: fighting, battling

with their joint applications: with their added requests

for their importunities: for pestering him in such a manner

mortal: fatal, deadly

challenged part of the honour: took some credit for the deed

for their vain covetousness of honour: as their reward for wanting a share in the "honour"

testament: will

firebrands: torches

People

Tillius Cimber: in Shakespeare's play, he is named Metellus Cimber.

Casca: Publius Servilius Casca Longus (see introductory notes)

Octavius Caesar: later called Caesar Augustus

Historic Occasions

March 15, 44 B.C.: The Ides of March (the death of Julius Caesar)

October, 42 B.C.: the deaths of Cassius and Brutus

Reading

Part One

Certainly, destiny may easier be foreseen than avoided: considering the strange and wonderful signs that were said to be seen before Caesar's death. As to the lights in the heavens, the noises heard in the night, and the wild birds which perched in the Forum, these are not perhaps worth taking notice of in so great a case as this. Strabo, the philosopher, tells us that a number of men were seen, looking as if they were heated through with fire, **contending** with each other; that a quantity of flame issued from the hand of a soldier's servant, so that they who saw it thought he must be burnt, but that after all he had no hurt. As Caesar was sacrificing, the victim's heart was missing, a very bad omen, because no living creature can subsist without a heart.

Furthermore, there was a certain soothsayer that had given Caesar warning long time afore, to take heed of the day of the Ides of March (which is the fifteenth of the month), for on that day he should be in great danger. That day being come, Caesar going unto the Senate house, and speaking merrily to the soothsayer, told him. "The Ides of March be come." "So be they," softly answered the soothsayer, "but yet are they not past." And the very day before, Caesar supping with Marcus Lepidus *[omission]*, and talk falling out amongst them, reasoning what death was best: he, preventing their opinions, cried out aloud, "Death unlooked for."

[Omission for length: Caesar's wife Calpurnia is reported to have dreamed of his death. Since she was not normally a superstitious woman, Caesar agreed to inquire of the soothsayers, and they agreed that the omens were not good. He decided to request that that day's meeting of the Senate be postponed. However, Decius Brutus Albinus, who was part of the conspiracy, came to Caesar's house and convinced him that he needed to attend the Senate.]

So Caesar coming into the house, all the Senate stood up on their feet to do him honour. Then part of Brutus's company and confederates stood round about Caesar's chair, and part of them also came towards him, pretending to add their petitions to those of **Tillius Cimber**, on behalf of his brother who was in exile; and they followed him **with their joint applications** till he came to his seat. When he was sat down, he refused to comply with their requests, and upon their urging him further began to reproach them severely **for their importunities**; when Tillius, laying hold of his robe with both his hands, pulled it down from his neck, was the signal for the assault.

Then **Casca** behind him struck him in the neck with his sword: howbeit the wound was not great nor **mortal**, because it seemed, the fear of such a devilish attempt did amaze him, and take his strength from him, that he killed him not at the first blow. But Caesar turning straight unto him, caught hold of his sword, and held it hard: and they both cried out, Caesar in Latin: "O vile traitor Casca, what doest thou?" and Casca in Greek to his brother, "Brother, help me."

At the beginning of this stir, they that were present, not knowing of the conspiracy, were so amazed with the horrible sight they saw, that they had no power to flee, neither to help him, not so much as once to make any outcry. They on the other side that had conspired his death, compassed him in on every side with their swords drawn in their hands, so that Caesar turned him nowhere, but he was stricken at by some, and still had naked swords in his face, and was hacked and mangled among them, as a wild beast taken of hunters. For it was agreed among them that every man should give him a wound, because all their parts should be in this murder. Men report also, that Caesar did still defend himself against the rest, running every way with his body: but when he saw Brutus with his sword drawn in his hand, then he pulled his gown over his head, and made no more resistance *[omission]*.

Part Two

When Caesar was slain, Brutus stood forth to give a reason for what they had done, but the Senate would not hear him: they flew out of doors in all haste, and fleeing, filled all the city with marvellous fear and tumult. Insomuch as some did shut their doors, others forsook their shops and warehouses, and others ran to the place to see what the matter was: and others also that had seen it, ran home to their houses again. But Antony and Lepidus, which were two of Caesar's chiefest friends, got off privately, and hid themselves in some friends' houses.

Brutus and his confederates, on the other side, being yet hot with this murder they had committed, having their swords drawn in their hands, came all in a troop together out of the Senate, and went into the Forum, not as men that made countenance to flee, but otherwise boldly holding up their heads like men of courage, and called to the people to defend their liberty, and stayed to speak with every great personage whom they met in their way. Of them, some followed this troop, and went amongst them, as if they had been of the conspiracy, and falsely **challenged part of the honour** with them: among them were Gaius Octavius and Lentulus Spinther. But both of them were afterwards put to death, **for their vain covetousness of honour**, by Antony and **Octavius Caesar**; and yet they had no part of that honour for the which they were put to death, neither did any man believe that they were any of the confederates, or of counsel with them. For neither did those who punished them profess to revenge the fact, but the ill-will.

Part Three

The next morning, Brutus and his confederates came into the Forum to speak unto the people, who listened without expressing either any pleasure or resentment, but showed by their silence that they pitied Caesar and respected Brutus. Now the Senate granted general pardon for all that was past; and to pacify every man. They ordered that Caesar should be worshipped as a divinity, and nothing, even of the slightest consequence, should be revoked which he had enacted during his governmcnt. At thc same time they gave Brutus and his followers the command of provinces, and other considerable posts: whereby every man thought all things were brought to good peace and quietness again.

But when they had opened Caesar's **testament**, and found a liberal legacy of money bequeathed unto every citizen of Rome; and that they saw his body (which was brought into the Forum) all bemangled with gashes of swords; then there was no order to keep the multitude and common people quiet, but they plucked up benches, tables, and stools, and laid them all about the body, and setting them afire, burnt the corpse. Then when the fire was well kindled, they took the **firebrands**, and went unto the houses of those that had slain Caesar, to set them afire. Other also ran up and down the city to see if they could meet with any of them, to cut them in pieces: howbeit they could meet with never a man of them, because they had locked themselves up safely in their houses.

There was one of Caesar's friends called Cinna, that had a marvellous strange and terrible dream the night before. He dreamed that Caesar bade him to supper, and that he refused, and would not go; then that Caesar took him by the hand, and led him against his will. Now Cinna hearing at that time, that they burnt Caesar's body, notwithstanding that he feared his dream, and though he was suffering from a fever, he went into the Forum to honour his funerals. When he came thither, one of mean sort asked what his name was? He was straight called by his name. The first man told it to another, and that other unto another, so that it ran straight through them all, that he was one of them that murdered Caesar (for indeed one of the traitors to Caesar, was also called Cinna as himself); wherefore, taking him for Cinna the murderer, they fell upon him with such fury, that they presently slew him *[omission]*.

This stir and fury made Brutus and Cassius more afraid than of all that was past; and therefore within a few days after, they departed out of Rome: and touching their doings afterwards, and what calamity they suffered till their deaths, we have written it at large, in the *Life of Brutus*.

Epilogue

Caesar died at fifty-six years of age: and Pompey also lived not passing four years more than he. So he reaped no other fruit of all his reign and dominion, which he had so vehemently desired all his life, and pursued with such extreme danger: but a vain name only, and a superficial glory, that procured him the envy and hatred of his country. But his great prosperity and good fortune that favoured him all his lifetime did continue afterwards in the revenge of his death, pursuing through every sea and land all those who were concerned in it, and suffering none to escape, but reaching all who in any sort or kind were either actually engaged in the fact, or by their counsels any way promoted it.

Furthermore, of all the chances that happen unto men upon the earth, that which came to Cassius above all others is most to be wondered at. For he, being overcome in battle at the journey of Philippi, slew himself with the same sword with which he struck Caesar.

Again, of signs in the element, the great comet which seven nights together was seen very bright after Caesar's death, the eighth night after was never seen more. Also the brightness of the sun was darkened, the which all that year through rose very pale, and shined not out, whereby it gave but small heat: therefore the air being very cloudy and dark, by the weakness of the heat that could not come forth, did cause the earth to bring forth but raw and unripe fruit, which rotted before it could ripen.

But above all, the ghost that appeared unto Brutus showed plainly that the gods were offended with the murder of Caesar. The vision was thus: Brutus being ready to pass over his army from the city of Abydos, to the other coast lying directly against it, slept every night (as his manner was) in his tent, and being yet awake, thinking of his affairs: (for by report he was as careful a captain, and lived with as little sleep, as ever man did) he thought he heard a noise at his tent door, and looking towards the light of the lamp that waxed very dim, he saw a horrible vision of a man, of a wonderful greatness, and dreadful look, which at the first made him marvellously afraid. But when he saw that it did him no hurt, but stood by his bedside, and said nothing: at length he asked him what he was. The image answered him: "I am thy ill angel, Brutus, and thou shalt see me by the city of Philippi." Then Brutus replied again, and said: "Well, I shall see thee then." Therewithal, the spirit presently vanished from him.

After that time Brutus being in battle near unto the city of Philippi, against Antony and Octavius Caesar, at the first battle he won the victory, and overthrowing all them that withstood him, he drove them into young Caesar's camp, which he took. The second battle being at hand, this spirit appeared again unto him, but spoke never a word. Thereupon Brutus knowing he should die, did put himself to all hazard in battle, but yet fighting could not be slain.

So seeing his men put to flight and overthrown, he ran unto a little rock not far off, and there setting his sword's point to his breast, fell upon it, and slew himself, but assisted, as they say, by a friend, who helped him to give the thrust, met his death.

Narration and Discussion

The story ends with Plutarch's pronouncement that "he reaped no other fruit of all his reign and dominion…but a vain name only, and a superficial glory, that procured him the envy and hatred of his country." Did Caesar end up with a vain name only?

Shakespeare turned his attention, at the end of the play, to Brutus, calling him "the noblest Roman of them all." In this *Life*, we have not heard much about Brutus, other than the fact that Caesar pardoned him for his support of Pompey. Is it surprising that Plutarch ended the story in this way?

Creative narration #1: Illustrate one event from this lesson.

Creative narration #2: Read the scenes from Shakespeare's play.

Shakespeare Connections

In Act I Scene I, we have the famous scene with the soothsayer: "Beware the Ides of March!" Act I Scene III begins on the evening before the murder, with **Casca**, breathless and fearful, describing some of the things he has seen. "Whoever knew the heavens menace so?" **Cassius** says to Casca that these natural or supernatural phenomena are all symbols of Caesar, "a man / Most like this dreadful night."

Acts II and III continue the story, and there are many points of comparison with Plutarch's text. Act IV begins with the dealings between Mark Antony, Octavius, and Lepidus; and then moves on to focus on Cassius and Brutus. The ghostly messenger ("the ghost of Caesar") appears to Brutus in Act IV, Scene III.

Cassius dies in Act V Scene III, and Brutus in Scene V. (Shakespeare added his own dramatic ending.)

Examination Questions

For younger students:

1. It is said that Caesar travelled continually and with great speed, and made little account of his diet. Tell two stories that illustrate this.

2. a) "I had rather be the chiefest man here, than the second person in Rome." b) "Fear not, for thou hast Caesar and his fortune with thee." On what occasions were these words used? Describe one of them.

For older students:

1. Write about **two** of the following, in connection with Julius Caesar: a), "He was not kept as a prisoner, but rather as a prince." (b) On his reading the history of Alexander. (c) "He fell into many thoughts with himself" when he came to the Rubicon. e) "[The soldiers at Brundisium] straight changed their complaints and minds."

2. (High school) "Now Caesar himself did breed the noble courage and life in [his soldiers]." Give a sketch of the character of Caesar as shown a) in this connection, b) in his dealings with Pompey.

Agis and Cleomenes
(Third Century B.C.)

"When the people heard what he said, they
marvelled much at the noble mind of this young
king, and were very glad of it, saying that for three
hundred years' space together, the city of Sparta
had not so worthy a king as he."

Popular images of cultures, peoples, and places do not always
recognize the effects of time and world events on those cultures.
School lessons on "Ancient Egypt," for example, might focus on the
age of Tutankhamun, in about 1300 B.C., but miss the point that the
Great Pyramid was built over a thousand years before that. Ancient
history, so to speak, to King Tut. "Ancient Rome" includes at least a
thousand years of change. A study of North American or British
culture over the past five hundred years would be meaningless without
an understanding of the events, discoveries, and shifts in government
that influenced daily life. Students in future centuries might envision a
Victorian-era man wearing a suit of armour, texting his friends about
enlisting in George Washington's army.

   When we study the Spartans, we often have an image of their
militaristic culture at its peak, around 600-400 B.C. Even Plutarch,

writing about that early age, describes them as a people raised in a kind of boot camp, whose ideal was to die gloriously in battle. The heroic deaths at Thermopylae took place in 480 B.C. By 404 B.C., Sparta had defeated Athens in the Second Peloponnesian War.

But Sparta's season of power was ending, and within a few years it was unexpectedly beaten in the landmark Battle of Leuctra with the Thebans. By the time the story of Agis and Cleomenes began, just over a hundred years later in 245 B.C., Sparta had become a different place. Ancient laws and traditions attributed to the (possibly mythical) lawgiver **Lycurgus (#1)** had been shoved aside. The rule that property must be inherited by family members, rather than bought or sold at will, was now irrelevant; the rich were getting richer by scooping up land. The majority of people living in the city were not Spartan citizens, so they had no particular interest in maintaining the old ideals of military discipline, or even in defending their state if it was threatened.

If the Spartans could have looked ahead another hundred years, they would have been even more shocked to know that all of Greece would be conquered by Rome. However, during the reigns of Agis and Cleomenes, Sparta hoped it still might be able to recover its old identity and power. The problem was how to go about it.

Why Agis (and Leonidas) *and* Cleomenes?

This *Life* is unusual because it includes the stories of two kings. (Dryden's translation separates the two, but North treats them as one.) The first few lessons are about Agis IV, the 25th king of the Eurypontid dynasty (see the chart below), and his co-ruler, Leonidas II, the 28th king of the Agiad dynasty. (A confusing point is that Agis, although his name sounds like he should be an Agiad, was a Eurypontid instead.) The second part is the story of the son and successor of Leonidas, Cleomenes III.

How was Sparta ruled? What was the Race of Hercules?

Sparta was ruled by two hereditary kings, one each from the Eurypontid and the Agiad dynasties (both of whom were supposed to be descended from Heracles/Hercules). The kings were assisted by the *Gerousia*, a council of elders ("old men") who were elected for life.

There were also five elected officials called **ephors**.

Two Spartan Dynasties
Eurypontid

Agis IV: succeeded his father as king in 245 B.C., and reigned four years before his death in 241 B.C.

Eudamidas III: son of Agis IV, a child king who "reigned" from 241 to 228 B.C. but who never really had power

Archidamus V: the brother of Agis IV; reigned from 228–227 B.C. (when he was assassinated)

Eucleidas or Euclidas: an Agiad by heredity, but he ruled (in the place of a Eurypontid king) with his brother Cleomenes until he was killed at the Battle of Sellasia.

Lycurgus (#2): not the lawgiver but a later Spartan king (219 B.C.)

Agiad

Leonidas II: reigned 254 to 235 B.C. Temporarily replaced by his son-in-law **Cleombrotus II**, who was afterwards sent into exile.

Cleomenes III: the son of Leonidas II, who succeeded him and reigned from 235–222 B.C. He seems to have been a bit younger than Agis, because in 241 B.C. he was considered slightly too young to marry.

Agesipolis III: the last of the Agiad kings, the grandson of Cleombrotus II. After the death of Cleomenes III, he became king while still a boy, but was soon deposed by Lycurgus #2 (see above).

Geography Notes

The **Peloponnesus** is the southern part of Greece; it is connected to the north by the **Isthmus of Corinth**. **Achaea** was both a territory on the northern coast of the Peloponnesus, and the name of an alliance of city-states in that region.

For our purposes, **Sparta (Spartan)** and **Lacedaemon (Lacedaemonian)** are synonymous. **Laconia** is the region in which Sparta/Lacedaemon was located, although Lacedaemon (or

Lacedaemonia) is used also to refer to the region rather than the city.

Laconic can mean anything in or of Laconia, but it also refers to Spartan traditions in clothing, diet, etc. A "Laconic answer" is brief, with no words wasted.

The region of **Arcadia** is in **Peloponnesus**, sometimes called **the Peloponnese**—the southern part of **Greece** that looks almost like a large island.

Macedon (or Macedonia) was an important kingdom to the north of Greece, but by this time it was struggling against the increasing power of the Achaean League.

Names That Are Easy to Confuse

Agis, **Agesilaus** [or **Agylaeus**]**(his uncle), **Archidamus** (his brother), **Agesistrata** (his mother), **Archidamia** (his grandmother), and **Agiatis** (his wife, later married to Cleomenes). Also **Aratus, Antigonus, Agesipolis,** and **Aristomachus.**

Cleombrotus vs. **Cleomenes**

Cratesiclea (mother of Cleomenes) vs. **Agesistrata** (mother of Agis)

Lycurgus vs. **Leonidas** vs. **Lysander** vs. **Lydiadas**

Top Vocabulary Terms

1. **commonwealth:** a state (such as Sparta) and its dependencies, possessions, provinces, and/or colonies

2. **ephor:** In addition to the kings and the *Gerousia* (see above), Sparta was ruled by five magistrates (elected officials), called ephors.

3. **horse:** soldiers on horseback; cavalry. The infantry, or foot soldiers, are sometimes referred to as **foot**.

4. **martial:** military

5. **mercenary:** working strictly for pay, i.e. as a soldier, and particularly those hired from another country. The word can be either an adjective or a noun ("The army was made up mostly of mercenaries"). North calls mercenaries "strangers."

6. **prefer:** propose

7. **sedition:** a treasonous plots or rebellion. Those who plot such things are **seditious**.

8. **strait:** narrow, strict

9. **succour, succours:** aid, help

10. **suffer:** allow

11. **talent:** a large amount of gold or silver

Lesson One

Introduction

In 245 B.C., the Greek city-state of Sparta had fallen into corruption. The Spartans had forgotten the laws set down for them by **Lycurgus (#1)**, including their style of dress and rules of inheritance. Traditionally, Spartan citizens could leave property only to their relatives, and this seemed to keep the economy stable and most people satisfied. Now properties were being bought and sold freely, causing some people to become very rich and others to fall into poverty. Could young King Agis convince everyone, including his co-ruler King Leonidas, to go back to the old ways?

Vocabulary

covetousness: wanting what one does not have; greed

voluptuousness and licentious life: unrestrained, self-indulgent behaviour

void: empty

Eurypontids, Agiads: see introductory notes

battle of Plataea: The final battle of the Persian Wars (323 B.C.)

magnanimity of mind: greatness of soul or spirit

spurn against: resist

in making himself fair: in other words, he did not do these things

houses: family groups or clans

ordinance: law

honest sciences: honourable pursuits

natural citizens of Sparta: members of the old Spartan families

no countenance nor calling: no wealth or honour (Dryden)

habituated and more confirmed in their vices: comfortable in their less-than-praiseworthy lifestyle

deploring: criticizing, finding unacceptable

prevailed with his uncle: had persuaded him to go along with his plan

strain her with great entreaty: plead with her

depart with her goods: give up her money or property

contempt: disregard

People

Agesilaus (#1): a former king of Sparta; the subject of one of Plutarch's *Lives*

Pausanias: a general and regent to the king, in the fifth century B.C.

Seleucus: Seleucus I Nicator was one of the generals of Alexander the Great, who (after Alexander's death) laid claim to a large piece of his empire, including the lands of Anatolia, Persia, and Mesopotamia. By the time Leonidas spent time in the royal court, it's likely that Seleucus had been succeeded by his son Antiochus I Soter.

Lycurgus (#1): the (possibly legendary) law-giver of Sparta

Lysander: not the famous general, just someone with the same name

Agesilaus (#2): sometimes spelled **Agylaeus**; the uncle of Agis and father of **Hippomedon**.

Ptolemy: the king of Egypt, probably Ptolemy III Euergetes

Historic Occasions

271 B.C.: Birth of Aratus (Achaean general)

c. 265 B.C.: Birth of Agis

c. 265-260 B.C.: Possible dates for the birth of Cleomenes

254 B.C.: Leonidas became the Agiad king of Sparta

251 B.C.: Formation of the Achaean League

251 B.C.: Aratus of Sicyon led a rebellion against Antigonus II Gonatas of Macedon (the king who fought against Pyrrhus)

245 B.C.: Agis became the Eurypontid king of Sparta

On the Map

Please review the Geography Notes in the introductory material.

Reading

Part One

[omission for length]

When the love of gold and silver crept again into the city of Sparta, and with riches, **covetousness** also and misery, and by use, **voluptuousness and licentious life**: Sparta was then **void** of all honour and goodness, and was for a long time drowned in shame and dishonour, until Kings Agis and Leonidas came to reign there.

Agis was of the house of the **Eurypontids**, the son of Eudamidas, the sixth of lineal descent after **Agesilaus (#1)**, who had been the greatest prince of all Greece in his time *[omission]*.

Leonidas also, the son of Cleonymus, was of the other family, the **Agiads**; he was the eighth of succession after **Pausanias**, who slew Mardonius, the king's lieutenant-general of Persia, in the **Battle of Plataea** *[omission]*. Howbeit his manners and conditions were never liked by the people. For though there was at that time in Sparta a general decline in manners, yet a greater revolt from the old habits appeared in him than in others. For he had lived a long time among the great lords of Persia, and followed also **Seleucus's** court, from whence he had brought all the pride and pomp of those courts into Greece, where law and reason ruleth.

Agis, on the contrary part, did not only far excel Leonidas in honour and **magnanimity of mind**: but all others almost also which had reigned in Sparta, from the time of Agesilaus the Great (#1). So that when Agis was not yet twenty years old, and being daintily brought up with the fineness of two women, his mother Agesistrata, and Archidamia his grandmother, which had more gold and silver than all the Lacedaemonians else: he began to **spurn against** these womanish delights and pleasures, such as **in making himself fair to be the better beliked**, and to be fine and trim in his apparel; and instead to cast upon him a plain Spartan cape, taking pleasure in the diet, baths, and manner of the ancient Laconian life: and he openly boasted besides, that he would not desire to be king, but only for the hope he had to restore the ancient Laconian life by his authority.

A Short Flashback

The Lacedaemonians might date the beginning of their corruption from their conquest of Athens, when they had stored both themselves and their country with plenty of gold and silver. Yet, nevertheless, the number of **houses** which **Lycurgus (#1)** appointed still being maintained, and the law remaining in force by which everyone was obliged to leave his lot or portion of land entirely to his son, a kind of order and equality was thereby preserved, which still in some degree sustained the state amidst its errors in other respects. This lasted until the time of the authority of Epitadeus, one of the ephors, a seditious man, and of proud conditions: who bitterly falling out with his own son, proposed a decree that all men should have liberty to dispose of their land by gift in their lifetime, or by their last will and testament. Thus this man made this law to satisfy his anger, and others also did confirm it for covetousness' sake, and so overthrew a noble **ordinance**. For the rich men then began to buy lands of numbers, and so transferred it from the right and lawful heirs: whereby a few men in short time being made very rich, immediately after there fell out great poverty in the city of Sparta, which made all **honest sciences** to cease, and brought in thereupon unlawful occupations; and the poor envied them that were wealthy. Therefore, there remained not above seven hundred **natural citizens of Sparta** in all, and of them, not above a hundred that had lands and inheritance: for all the rest were poor people in the city, and were of **no countenance nor calling**. Besides that, they went unwillingly to the wars against their enemies, looking every day for stir and change in the city.

Part Two

Agis therefore thinking it a notable good act (as indeed it was) to replenish the city of Sparta again, and to bring in the old equality, he moved the matter unto the citizens. He found the youth (against all hope) to give good ear unto him, and very well given unto virtue, easily changing their garments and life to recover their liberty again. But the old men, **habituated and more confirmed in their vices**, were most of them as alarmed at the very name of Lycurgus, as a fugitive slave to be brought back before his offended master. These men could not endure to hear Agis continually **deploring** the present state of Sparta, and wishing she might be restored to her ancient glory.

Howbeit **Lysander** the son of Libys, and Mandrocleides the son of Ecphanes, and **Agesilaus (#2)** also, greatly commended his noble desire, and persuaded him to go forward with it *[omission]*. Agesilaus was the king's uncle, by the mother's side; an eloquent man, but covetous and voluptuous, who was not moved by considerations of public good, but rather seemed to be persuaded in it by his son **Hippomedon**, whose courage and signal actions in war had gained him a high esteem and great influence among the young men of Sparta; though indeed the true motive was that he (Agesilaus) had many debts, and hoped by this means to be freed from them.

As soon as Agis had **prevailed with his uncle**, he sought by his means to gain his mother also, who had many friends and followers, and a number of persons in her debt in the city, and who took a considerable part in public affairs. At the first proposal she was very averse, and strongly advised her son not to engage in so difficult and so unprofitable an enterprise. But Agesilaus had told her what a notable act it would be, and how easily it might be brought to pass, with marvellous great profit; and King Agis began also to **strain her with great entreaty**, that she should willingly **depart with her goods** to win her son honour and glory. He told her he could not pretend to equal other kings in riches, the very followers and menials of the satraps and stewards of Seleucus or **Ptolemy** abounding more in wealth than all the Spartan kings put together; but if by **contempt** of wealth and pleasure, by simplicity and magnanimity, he could surpass their luxury and abundance; if he could restore their former equality to the Spartans; then he should be a great king indeed.

Narration and Discussion

How did the issue of property ownership create such a bad effect on the rest of Spartan life, such as causing "all honest sciences to cease?" (Is it wrong for people to buy land?)

Why did Agis believe that getting his people back "under the law" would actually be liberating for them? (Read Psalm 119:1-12.)

For older students and further thought (#1): Plutarch refers to the "womanish" upbringing of Agis, and his rebellion against it. This theme will come up in several other lessons as well: the Egyptians, in the final lessons, are viewed as "henpecked," and women who show unusual strength of character (such as the mother of Cleomenes) seem to do so in sad contrast to weaker male characters. Plutarch also seems to mildly disapprove of (or at least makes note of) the fact that Spartan women had financial power and were well-informed about government issues. Contrast his beliefs about gender with that of your own culture, and (for Christian students) with relevant Bible passages.

For older students (#2): Compare the strict Spartan laws laid out by

Lycurgus to those of the Israelites, especially regarding property inheritance, the Year of Jubilee, clothing, diet, and marriage to foreigners.

Hands-on narration: As an ongoing storytelling or narration tool for this study, you may want to create a graphic or hands-on illustration of the characters and their positions, beginning with the Spartans described in **Lesson One**. Use toothpick figures or small toy people to represent the characters, and place them on some type of a base such as a map, or a large piece of cardboard or poster board that can be marked as needed. As a beginning, you will want to mark off two small spaces within the boundaries of Sparta for the thrones of the Agiad and Eurypontid kings, and set the figures for Agis and Leonidas there. Add places near the thrones for five ephors, and perhaps a small group of figures to represent the council of the elders. You may want to create figures for the mother and grandmother of Agis, his wife Agiatis and his uncle Agesilaus (#2).

If it is not possible to create such a base, you could draw the characters on index cards, and simply add, group, or subtract them as needed.

Lesson Two

Introduction

Agis used his new power as king to propose a one-time cancellation of debts, and re-distribution of land among both the old families and those newcomers who were willing to fight for Sparta. To show his seriousness, Agis was the first to put his own land up for division. However, the elders and ephors (particularly those who had a lot of land or who were owed money) wanted to take things more slowly.

Vocabulary

impart to them…: tell them what was going on in the government

superfluous trifles: luxury goods

felicity: happiness; in this case, delight and joy

clean trodden underfoot: trampled on

rash: impulsive; showing a lack of consideration

alteration: a change in the way things were done

thwart: stop, ruin

usurp arbitrary power: take total control of the government

the council: the elders or *Gerousia* (see introductory notes)

patrimony: his inherited land

tillage: farmland

ready money: cash (vs. something promised for later)

indifferently: without exception

suppliant: one who pleads or begs for mercy

Temple of Athena: The Greek goddess Athena had a temple in Sparta, where she was called *Athena Khalkíoikos* (or Chalcioecus), which means "of the brazen (bronze) house."

cited: summoned; called to appear in court

vice: evil, sin

deeds of obligation: proof that money was owed

People

Cleombrotus: the son-in-law of Leonidas, who now became King Cleombrotus II

Historic Occasions

243 B.C.: The Macedonians lost the fortress called the Acrocorinth (with the result that **Corinth** joined the Achaean League)

c. 242 B.C.: Leonidas was exiled from Sparta

239 B.C.: Death of Antigonus II of Macedon

On the Map

Tegea: a town in **Arcadia**

Corinth: If students are unfamiliar with the city of Corinth, they should locate it (and the Isthmus of Corinth) on the map of Greece.

Reading

Part One

In conclusion, the mother and the grandmother also were so taken, so carried away with the inspiration, as it were, of the young man's noble and generous ambition, that they not only consented, but were ready on all occasions to spur him on; and not only sent to speak on his behalf with the men with whom they had an interest, but addressed the other women also, knowing well that the Lacedaemonian wives had always a great power with their husbands, who used to **impart to them their state affairs** with greater freedom than the women would communicate with the men in the private business of their families. Which was indeed one of the greatest obstacles to this design: for the money of Sparta being most of it in the women's hands, it was their interest to oppose it, not only as depriving them of those **superfluous trifles**, in which, through want of better knowledge and experience, they placed all their **felicity**; but also, because they saw their honour and authority which they had by their riches, **clean trodden underfoot**.

Therefore they coming to Leonidas, they did persuade him to reprove Agis, because he was an elder man than he, and to put a stop to the ill-advised projects of a **rash** young man. Leonidas did what he could in favour of the rich; but fearing the common people, who desired nothing but **alteration**, he dared not openly speak against him, but underhand he did all he could to discredit and **thwart** the project, and to prejudice the chief magistrates against him; and on all occasions he craftily insinuated that it was at the price of letting him **usurp arbitrary power** that Agis thus proposed to divide the property of the rich among the poor, and that the object of these measures for cancelling debts and dividing the lands was not to furnish Sparta with citizens but to purchase him a tyrant's bodyguard.

This notwithstanding, King Agis having procured Lysander to be chosen one of the ephors, he presently preferred his law unto **the council**:

> That such as were in debt should be cleared of all
> their debts; and that the lands also should be
> divided into equal parts; so that from the Valley of
> Pallena unto Mount Taugetus, and unto the cities of
> Malea and Sellasia, there should be four thousand
> five hundred parts; and without those bounds, there
> should be in all the rest, fifteen thousand parts, the
> which should be distributed unto their neighbours
> who were able to carry weapons; and the rest unto
> the natural Spartans. The number of them should
> be replenished with their neighbours and strangers
> in like manner, which should be very well brought
> up, and be able men besides to serve the
> commonwealth: all the which afterwards should be
> divided into fifteen companies, of the which, some
> should receive two hundred, and others four
> hundred men, and should live according to the old
> ancient institution observed by their ancestors.

This law being proposed in the council of the elders met there with opposition; whereupon Lysander himself assembled the great council of all the people, and there spoke unto them himself, and Mandrocleides and Agesilaus (#2) also, praying them not to suffer the honour of Sparta to be trodden underfoot for the vanity of a few *[omission]*. When every man else had spoken, King Agis rising up, briefly speaking unto the people, said that he would bestow great contributions for the reformation of this commonwealth, which he was desirous to restore again. For first of all, he would divide among them all his **patrimony**, which was of large extent in **tillage** and pasture; he would also give six hundred talents in **ready money**, and his mother, grandmother, and his other friends and relations, who were the richest of the Lacedaemonians, were ready to follow his example.

When the people heard what he said, they marvelled much at the noble mind of this young king, and were very glad of it, saying that for three hundred years' space together, the city of Sparta had not so worthy a king as he. But Leonidas contrarily assayed with all his power he could to resist him, thinking with himself that if King Agis's purpose took place, he should also be compelled to contribute money, and yet he should have no thanks, but King Agis would: because that all the Spartans **indifferently** should be compelled to make their goods in common, but the honour should be his only that first began it.

[Omission: the elders debated the proposal, but it was defeated by one vote.]

Part Two

Wherefore Lysander, who was yet in office, attempted to accuse Leonidas by an ancient law, forbidding that none of the race of Hercules should marry with any foreign woman, nor beget children of her: because he had married a woman in Asia, and had two children by her; and afterwards being forsaken by her, he returned again into his country against his will, and so had possessed the kingdom for lack of lawful heir *[omission]*. So following his accusation in this manner, Lysander persuaded **Cleombrotus** to lay claim to the kingdom. He was of the royal family, and son-in-law to Leonidas; who, fearing now the event of this process, fled as a **suppliant** to the **Temple of Athena**, together with his daughter, the wife of Cleombrotus; for she in this occasion resolved to leave her husband, and to follow her father. Leonidas then being **cited**, and not appearing, they deposed him and made Cleombrotus king.

Part Three

Soon after this revolution, Lysander concluded his year in office, and new ephors were chosen, who gave Leonidas assurance of safety; and cited Lysander and Mandrocleides to answer for having, contrary to law, cancelled debts, and designed a new division of lands.

[Omission for length: Lysander and Mandrocleides, seeing they were in trouble,

went to the kings and pleaded for them to act together to resist the ephors. The kings began to do just that: they replaced the ephors with their own supporters, including Agesilaus (#2), and released many prisoners. Agesilaus used his new power to attempt to kill Leonidas as he fled to **Tegea***, but King Agis heard of the plot in time and made sure that Leonidas arrived safely.]*

Thus their purpose taking effect, and no man contrarying them: one man only, Agesilaus, overthrew all, and dashed a noble Laconian law by a shameful **vice**, which was covetousness. For he, having the best lands of any man in the country, and owing a great sum of money besides, would neither pay his debts, nor let go his land. Therefore he persuaded Agis that if both these things should be put in execution at the same time, so great and so sudden an alteration might cause some dangerous commotion; but if debts were in the first place cancelled, the rich men would afterwards more easily be prevailed with to part with their land.

Lysander was also of this opinion, being deceived in like manner by the craft of Agesilaus: so that all men were presently commanded to bring in their bonds, or **deeds of obligation**, which the Lacedaemonians called *claria*, into the marketplace, where being laid together in a heap, they set fire to them. The wealthy, money-lending people, one may easily imagine, beheld it with a heavy heart; but Agesilaus, mocking them, said he never saw a brighter fire in his life.

Narration and Discussion

Why was King Leonidas so resistant to Agis's proposals?

How (and why) did Agesilaus deceive Agis and Lysander?

Hands-on narration: Continuing from the activity begun in **Lesson One**, you might add the state of Macedon and its king. You will also need to move King Leonidas to the city of Tegea, and put Cleombrotus on that throne instead. Think about ways that you could show groups of allied states, such as the Achaean and Aetolian Leagues. Would it work better to draw a line around them, or to add some kind of symbol (such as a coloured sticker) to show their loyalties?

Creative narration: Write or act out an interview with a wealthy creditor in Sparta. A possible question: Although you will lose money if all debts are cancelled, would you be willing to accept these reforms for the sake of restoring the old Spartan values?

Lesson Three

Introduction

The Spartans demanded that the lands should be divided as they had agreed, but Agesilaus (#2) found reasons to delay this. At this time also, King Agis led an army to Corinth to help prevent an invasion by the Aetolians, and "shewed himself in his counsel, then no rash, but a resolute and valiant man" (North's phrase). But when Agis returned home, he found Sparta "in great broil and trouble."

Vocabulary

an immediate division of lands: as they had been promised

in virtue of a defensive treaty of alliance: because the Spartans had agreed to send help if they were attacked

hinder this incursion: stop this invasion

auxiliaries: military troops, but not the main part of the army; often made up of mercenary soldiers

with wonderful alacrity: enthusiastically

discourse: converse, talk

fare hardly: live the rough life of a soldier

habit: dress

to their prejudice: not in their best interest

expedient: practical; a good idea

temerity or presumption: arrogance

imminent: about to happen

insolent: arrogant, sure of himself

contemned: scoffed at

highly incensed: very angry

sanctuary: place of safety

get him thence: go away from there

vainglory: selfish ambition

hypocrisy: saying you believe one thing, but doing the opposite

malefactors: criminals

believe in other men's professions: trust what others said

People

Aratus: Aratus of Sicyon, who was elected *strategos* (general) of the **Achaean League** seventeen times

Historic Occasions

242 B.C.: Leonidas was exiled

Summer, 241 B.C.: Spartan troops were sent to aid the Achaeans in defending the Peloponnesus against an Aetolian invasion. Because Agis and Aratus could not seem to agree on a strategy, the Spartans went home again, with their alliance at an end.

241 B.C.: Death of Agis

On the Map

Aetolians, Aetolian League: a confederation of Greek states that stood in opposition to Macedon and the **Achaean League**

Megara: a town in Greece, in the northern part of the **Isthmus of Corinth**, across from the island of **Salamis**

Reading

Part One

And now the people pressed earnestly for **an immediate division of lands**; the kings also had ordered it should be done; but Agesilaus (#2), sometimes pretending one difficulty, and sometimes another, delayed the execution, till an occasion happened to call Agis to the wars. The Achaeans, **in virtue of a defensive treaty of alliance,** sent to demand succours, as they expected every day that the **Aetolians** would attempt to enter Peloponnesus from the territory of **Megara**. They had sent **Aratus**, their general, to collect forces to **hinder this incursion**. Aratus wrote to the ephors, who immediately gave order that Agis should hasten to their assistance with the Spartan **auxiliaries**.

Agis was extremely pleased to see the zeal and bravery of those who went with him upon this expedition. They were for the most part young men, and poor; and being just released from their debts and set at liberty, and hoping on their return to receive each man his lot of land, they followed their king **with wonderful alacrity**. The cities through which they passed were in admiration to see how they marched from one end of Peloponnesus to the other, without the least disorder, and, in a manner, without being heard. It gave the Greeks occasion to **discourse** with one another, how great might be the temperance and modesty of a Laconian army in old time, under their famous captains Agesilaus (#1), Lysander, or Leonidas, since they saw such discipline and exact obedience under a leader who perhaps was the youngest man in all the army. They saw also how he was himself content to **fare hardly**, ready to undergo any labours, and not to be distinguished by pomp or richness of **habit** or arms from the meanest of his soldiers; and to people in general it was an object of regard and admiration. But rich men viewed the innovation with dislike and alarm, lest haply the example might spread, and work changes **to their prejudice** in their own countries as well.

Agis joined Aratus near the city of Corinth, where it was still a matter of debate whether or no it were **expedient** to give the enemy battle. Agis, on this occasion, showed great forwardness and resolution, yet without **temerity or presumption**. He declared it was his opinion they ought to fight, thereby to hinder the enemy from passing the gates of Peloponnesus; but nevertheless he would submit to the judgment of Aratus, not only as the elder and more experienced captain, but as he was general of the Achaeans, whose forces he would not pretend to command, but was only come thither to assist them.

[Omission for length: Plutarch explains that there was some question about which of the generals did want to go ahead, and which one wanted to hold off; but, however it happened, it was mutually agreed to end their alliance. The Spartans went home, and Aratus's troops ended up fighting the Aetolians themselves.]

Part Two

Agis, not without having gained a great deal of honour, returned to Sparta, where he found the people in great broil and trouble, and a new revolution **imminent**. For Agesilaus (#2), now being one of the ephors, finding himself rid of the fear which before kept him under some restraint, cared not what injury or mischief he did to any citizen, so he might get money. Among other things, he exacted a thirteenth month's tax, whereas the usual cycle required at this time no such addition to the year. For these and other reasons, fearing those whom he injured, and knowing how he was hated by the people, he thought it necessary to maintain a guard, which always accompanied him to the magistrate's office. And presuming now on his power, he was grown so **insolent**, that of the two kings, the one he openly **contemned**; and if he showed any respect towards Agis, would have thought it rather an effect of his near relationship, than any duty or submission to the royal authority. He gave it out also that he was to continue as ephor the ensuing year.

His enemies, therefore, alarmed by this report, lost no time in risking an attempt against him; and, openly bringing back Leonidas from Tegea, they re-established him in the kingdom, to which even the people, **highly incensed** for having been defrauded in the promised division of lands, willingly consented. Agesilaus himself would hardly have escaped their fury, if his son Hippomedon, whose manly virtues made him dear to all, had not saved him out of their hands, and then privately conveyed him from the city.

Part Two

During the commotion, the two kings fled: Agis to the Temple of Athena, and Cleombrotus to that of Neptune. For Leonidas was more incensed against his son-in-law; and leaving Agis alone, went with his soldiers to Cleombrotus's **sanctuary**, and there with great passion reproached him for having, though he was son-in-law, conspired with his enemies, usurped his throne, and forced him from his country. Cleombrotus, having little to say for himself, sat silent.

His wife, Chilonis, the daughter of Leonidas, had chosen to follow her father in his sufferings; for when Cleombrotus usurped the kingdom, she forsook him, and wholly devoted herself to comfort her father in his affliction; whilst he still remained in Sparta, she remained also, as a suppliant, with him; and when he fled, she fled with him, bewailing his misfortune, and extremely displeased with Cleombrotus.

But now, upon this turn of fortune, she changed in like manner; and was seen sitting now as a suppliant with her husband, embracing him with her arms, and having her two little children beside her. All men wondering, and weeping for pity to see the goodness and natural love of this lady, who, showing her mourning apparel, and the hair of her head flaring about her eyes, bareheaded, spoke in this sort:

> "O father mine, this sorrowful garment and
> countenance is not for pity of Cleombrotus, but hath
> long remained with me, lamenting sore your former
> misery and exile: but now, which of the two should I
> rather choose, either to continue a mourner in this
> pitiful state, seeing you again restored to your
> kingdom, having overcome your enemies; or else
> putting on my princely apparel, to see my husband
> slain, unto whom you married me as a maid? Who,
> if he cannot move you to take compassion of him,
> and to obtain mercy, by the tears of his wife and
> children: he shall then abide more bitter pain of his
> evil counsel, than that which you intend to make
> him suffer..."

[omission]

Leonidas after he had talked a little with his friends, commanded Cleombrotus to **get him thence**, and to leave the city as an exile; and prayed his daughter for his sake to remain with him, and not to forsake her father, that did so dearly love her, as for her sake he had saved her husband's life. This notwithstanding, she would not yield to his request, but rising up with her husband, gave him one of his sons, and herself took the other in her arms: and then making her prayer before the altar of the goddess, she went as a banished woman away with her husband. And truly the example of her virtue was so famous, that if Cleombrotus's mind had not been too much blinded with **vainglory**, he had cause to think his exile far more happy, to enjoy the love of so noble a wife as he had, than for the kingdom which he possessed without her.

Part Three

[Omission for length: Finding it impossible to persuade Agis to leave his sanctuary, Leonidas decided to trap him instead. Some of his friends offered him their protection if he would go to the public baths with them; but one of them, having a personal grudge, betrayed Agis on the way back, and he was taken to prison.]

None of Agis's friends being near to assist him, or anyone by, they therefore easily got him into the prison, where Leonidas was already arrived, with a company of soldiers who strongly guarded all the avenues; the ephors also came in, with as many of the elders as they knew to be true to their party, being desirous to proceed with some semblance of justice. And thus they bade him give an account of his actions. The young man laughed at their **hypocrisy**. But Amphares told him that it was no laughing sport, and that he should pay for his folly. Another of the ephors, as though he would be more favourable, and offering as it were an excuse, asked him whether he was not forced to what he did by Agesilaus and Lysander. But Agis answered he had not been constrained by any man, nor had any other intent in what he did but only to follow the example of Lycurgus (#1), and to govern conformably to his laws.

Then the same ephor asked him again, if he did not repent him of that he had done. The young man boldly answered him, that he would never repent him of so wise and virtuous an enterprise, though he ventured his life for it. Then they condemned him to death, and bade the officers carry him to the Dechas, as it is called, a place in the prison where they strangle **malefactors**. And when the officers would not venture to lay hands on him, and the very mercenary soldiers declined it, believing it an illegal and a wicked act to lay violent hands on a king, Demochares, threatening and reviling them for it, himself thrust him into the room.

Now the rumour ran straight through the city, that King Agis was taken; and a multitude of people were at the prison doors with lights and torches. Thither came also Agis' mother and grandmother, shrieking out, and praying that the King of Sparta might yet be heard and judged by the people. For this cause, they hastened his death the sooner, and were afraid besides, lest the people in the night would take him out of their hands by force, if there came any more people thither.

Thus King Agis, being led to his death, spied a sergeant lamenting and weeping for him, unto whom he said: "Good fellow, I pray thee weep not for me, for I am honester man than they that so shamefully put me to death," and with those words he willingly put his head into the halter.

[The mother and grandmother of King Agis were put to death as well.]

So wicked and barbarous an act had never been committed in Sparta since first the Dorians inhabited Peloponnesus *[omission]*. Be it as it will, it is certain at least that Agis was the first king put to death in Lacedaemon by the ephors, for having undertaken a design noble in itself and worthy of his country, at a time of life when men's errors usually meet with an easy pardon. And if errors he did commit, his enemies certainly had less reason to blame him than had his friends for that gentle and compassionate temper which made him save the life of Leonidas, and **believe in other men's professions**.

Narration and Discussion

If you had been Chilonis, the daughter of Leonidas, would you have stayed in Sparta with him, or gone into exile with your husband?

How did Agis demonstrate courage during his trial?

Hands-on narration: Use your models to show any of the following: the Aetolian invasion, adding the new figure of the Achaean general Aratus; the flight of the two kings to nearby temples; the return of Leonidas; the exile of Cleombrotus; the death of Agis.

Creative narration: Write a conversation between either a) Agesilaus and his son Hippomedon, or b) Cleombrotus and Chilonis.

Lesson Four

Introduction

In this lesson we meet Cleomenes, first as a young prince of Sparta, and then as king. Forced to marry the widow of Agis, he had the opportunity to hear the whole story from the inside out.

It's important to notice here that alliances in the Greek world were changing. Sparta had previously supported the Achaean League, or at least tried to (Lesson Three), but when the Spartan ephors ordered Cleomenes to seize the Athenaeum, a fortress near a disputed boundary, the Achaeans saw it as an act of war, and responded in kind.

Vocabulary

mother of a young child: Eudamidas III, next in line for the Agiad throne, but due to his age (he was only a baby at the time) he never officially reigned. He died in 228 B.C.

in fancy with her: in love with her

temperance and moderation of life: without extremes such as excessive spending or drinking

scrupulous, circumspect, and gentle: Scrupulous can refer to one's attention to detail, or more generally to upholding values such as honesty. Cleomenes lacked Agis's strong sense of honour, and his willingness to put his country above his own interests. **Circumspect**

means cautious, unwilling to take risks; Cleomenes was a little more impulsive than Agis, and he was less gentle when it came to "making" people do what he thought was right.

disputation: formal debate

dissolute: lacking in morals

the posture of affairs: the way things were going

frantic: obsessed with this idea

fair occasions: legitimate reasons

despising Cleomenes…: Aratus was about ten years older than Cleomenes.

cockerel: young rooster

People

Archidamus: see introductory notes. After the young son of Agis, he was next in line to the Agiad throne.

Sphaerus: a Stoic philosopher

Zeno of Citium: founder of the Stoic school of philosophy

Historic Occasions

235 B.C.: Cleomenes III became the Agiad king of Sparta (after the death of Leonidas); he was probably between 25 to 30 years old

229/228 B.C.-222 B.C.: Cleomenean War between Sparta and the Achaean League

On the Map

Belbina: or Belemina; a town near the northwest border of Laconia

Megalopolis (Megalopolitans): a city in Arcadia (see **Lesson Five**)

Orchomenus: a city in Arcadia

Reading

Part One

Thus fell Agis. His brother **Archidamus** was too quick for Leonidas, and saved himself by a timely retreat. But Agis's wife Agiatis, then **mother of a young child**, he forced from her own house, and compelled to marry his son Cleomenes, who was yet underage to marry: fearing lest this young lady should be bestowed elsewhere, being indeed a great heir, and of a rich house, and the daughter of Gylippus; besides that she was the fairest woman at that time in all Greece, and well-conducted in her habits of life. And therefore, they say, she did all she could that she might not be compelled to this new marriage.

But now being at length married unto Cleomenes, she ever hated Leonidas to the death, and yet was a good and loving wife unto her young husband: who immediately after he was married unto her, fell greatly **in fancy with her**, and for compassion's sake (as it seemed) he thanked her for the love she bore unto her first husband, and for the loving remembrance she had of him: insomuch as he himself many times would fall in talk of it, and would be inquisitive how things had passed, taking great pleasure to hear of Agis's wise counsel and purpose. For Cleomenes was as desirous of honour, and had as noble a mind as Agis, and was born also to **temperance and moderation of life**, as Agis in like manner was, but **not so scrupulous, circumspect, and gentle**. There was something of heat and passion always goading him on, and an impetuosity and violence in his eagerness to pursue anything which he thought good and just. To have men obey him of their own freewill, he conceived to be the best discipline; but likewise, to subdue resistance, and force them to the better course was, in his opinion, commendable and brave.

Furthermore, the manners of the citizens of Sparta, giving themselves over to idleness and pleasure, he did not like at all. The king let everything take its own way, thankful if nobody gave him any disturbance, nor called him away from the enjoyment of his wealth and luxury. The public interest was neglected, and each man was intent upon his private gain. It was dangerous, now Agis was killed, so much as to name such a thing as the exercising and training of their youth; and to speak of the ancient temperance, endurance, and equality was a sort of treason against the state.

They say also, that Cleomenes, whilst a boy, had heard some **disputation** of philosophy, when the philosopher **Sphaerus**, of the country of Borysthenes, came to Lacedaemon, and spent some time and trouble in instructing the youth. He was one of the chiefest scholars of **Zeno of Citium**, and delighted (as it seemed) in Cleomenes' noble mind, and had a great desire to prick him forward unto honour.

Part Two

Upon the death of his father Leonidas, Cleomenes was come unto the crown; and observing the citizens of Sparta at that time were very **dissolute**, that the rich men followed their pleasure and profit taking no care of the commonwealth, that the poor men also for very want and need went with no good life and courage to the wars, neither cared for the bringing up of their children; and that he himself had but the name of a king, and the ephors all the power: he was resolved to change **the posture of affairs**. He had a friend named Xenares *[omission for content]*, of whom he would commonly inquire what manner of king Agis was, by what means and by what assistance he began and pursued his designs. Xenares, at first, willingly complied with his request, and told him the whole story, with all the particular circumstances of the actions. But when he observed Cleomenes to be extremely affected at the relation, and more than ordinarily taken with Agis's new model of the government, and begging a repetition of the story, he at first scolded him, told him he was **frantic**, and at last left off all sort of familiarity *[omission]*; yet he never told any man the cause of their disagreement, but would only say, Cleomenes knew very well.

Cleomenes, finding Xenares averse to his designs, and thinking all others to be of the same disposition, consulted with none, but contrived the whole business by himself. And considering that it would be easier to bring about an alteration when the city was at war than when in peace, he engaged the commonwealth in a quarrel with the Achaeans, who had given them **fair occasions** to complain. For Aratus, a man of the greatest power amongst all the Achaeans, designed from the very beginning to bring all the Peloponnesians into one common body. And to effect this was the one object of all his many commanderships and his long political course, as he thought this the only means to make them a match for their foreign enemies. Pretty nearly all the rest agreed to his proposals; only the Lacedaemonians, the Eleans, and as many of the Arcadians as inclined to the Spartan interest, remained unpersuaded.

And so, as soon as Leonidas was dead, Aratus began to invade the cities of Arcadia, and wasted those especially that bordered on Achaea; by this means designing to try the inclinations of the Spartans, and **despising Cleomenes as a youth**, and of no experience in affairs of state or war. Thereupon the ephors sent Cleomenes to surprise the Athenaeum, near **Belbina**, which is a pass commanding an entrance into Laconia; howbeit the place at that time was in question betwixt the **Megalopolitans** and the Lacedaemonians. Cleomenes possessed himself of the place, and fortified it; at which action Aratus showed no public resentment, but marched by night to surprise Tegea and **Orchomenus**.

The design failed, for those that were to betray the cities into his hands turned afraid; so Aratus retreated, imagining that his design had been undiscovered. But Cleomenes wrote a sarcastic letter to him, and desired to know, as from a friend, whither he intended to march at night. Aratus returned answer again that, understanding Cleomenes meant to fortify Belbina, he meant to march thither to oppose him. Cleomenes rejoined that he did not dispute it, but begged to be informed, if he might be allowed to ask the question, why he carried those torches and ladders with him. Aratus laughed at the jest, and asked what manner of youth this was. Democritus, a Spartan exile, answered; "If thou hast anything to do against the Lacedaemonians, thou hadst need make haste, before this young **cockerel** have on his spurs." *[Dryden uses a different metaphor: "begin before this young eagle's talons are grown."]*

Narration and Discussion

Describe the unexpected outcome of the marriage between Agiatis and Cleomenes.

What impression did General Aratus get of his enemy Cleomenes during these events?

Hands-on narration: Cleomenes is now on one of the Spartan thrones; the other is occupied by the young son of Agis. This would be a good time to add Arcadia, including the large city of Megalopolis.

Creative narration: Write a letter or a diary entry by a Spartan citizen, describing life under Leonidas.

Lesson Five

Introduction

The war had officially begun between Sparta and the Achaean League; but wars are expensive, and Cleomenes needed to convince the Spartans that it would be worthwhile in the end. After unsuccessfully attempting to bring back the brother of Agis, he realized that the real power lay with the five ephors.

Vocabulary

they commissioned him again: they ordered him to continue fighting

cowed: intimidated, scared

he put a strong garrison into it: he fortified it with soldiers

called to an account: made to answer for the murder of Agis

sift: test

furnished Orchomenus with provisions: brought in food for the citizens of the town, which was under siege by the Achaeans

so harassed the Lacedaemonians: Cleomenes seemed to be attempting to either get the "naysayers" killed in these battles, or wear them out so that they wouldn't interfere with his plan.

People

Lydiadas: The former ruler of Megalopolis, elected *strategos* or general of the **Achaean League** in three different years. In 227 B.C., he ran again for *strategos* but was defeated by **Aratus**, and was chosen *hipparch* (cavalry commander) instead.

Aristomachus: Aristomachus (or Aristomachos) of Argos, the newly-elected *strategos* of the Achaean League

Agesilaus (#2): the uncle of Agis (**Lesson Two**)

Historic Occasions

228 B.C.: Death of Eudamidas III, the Eurypontid king

228/227 B.C.: Accession and death of Archidamus V

227 B.C.: Battle of Mount Lycaeum; death of Lydiadas

On the Map

Caphyae: a city of **Arcadia**, northwest of the lake of **Orchomenus**

Methydrium: a town in central Arcadia

Argos (Argives): a city in the **Argolis** region of the Peloponnesus

Pallantium: a town west of **Tegea**

Elis (Eleans): a district of southern Greece

the mountain Lycaeum: or Lykaion; a mountain in Arcadia which was believed to be sacred to the god Zeus

Messene: a city-state in the Peloponnesus

Leuctra: a city in the territory of **Megalopolis**

Tarentum (Tarentines): or Tarento; a city in Apulia, Italy

Crete (Cretans): the largest of the Greek islands

Megalopolis: Megalopolis was the "big city" of mostly-rural **Arcadia**.

Mantinea, Heraea, Asea: cities/towns in Arcadia

Reading

Part One

Presently after this, Cleomenes, encamping in Arcadia with a few horse and three hundred foot, received orders from the ephors, who feared to engage in the war, commanding him to return home; but when upon his retreat Aratus took **Caphyae, they commissioned him again**. In this expedition he took **Methydrium**, and overran the country of the **Argives**; then the Achaeans, to oppose him, came out with an army of twenty thousand foot and one thousand horse, under the command of **Aristomachus**. Cleomenes faced them at **Pallantium**, and offered battle, but Aratus, being **cowed** by his bravery, would not suffer the general to engage; but retreated, amidst the reproaches of the Achaeans and the derision and scorn of the Spartans, who were not above five thousand.

Cleomenes' courage being now lifted up, and bravely speaking to his citizens: he reminded them of a saying of one of their ancient kings, that the Lacedaemonians never inquired what number their enemies were, but where they were.

Part Two

Shortly after, the Achaeans making war with the **Eleans**, Cleomenes was sent to aid them, and met with the army of the Achaeans by **the mountain Lycaeum** as they were in their return. He, setting upon them, gave them the overthrow, slew a great number of them, and took many also prisoners, so that the rumour ran through Greece, how Aratus himself was slain. Aratus, wisely taking the occasion which this victory gave him, went straight to the city of Mantinea, and taking it upon a sudden, when no man knew of his coming, **he put a strong garrison into it**.

Upon this, the Lacedaemonians being quite discouraged, and opposing Cleomenes' designs of carrying on the war, he now exerted himself to have Archidamus, the brother of Agis, sent for from **Messene**; as he, of the other family, had a right to the kingdom, and besides, Cleomenes thought that the power of the ephors would be reduced when the kingly state was thus filled up, and raised to its proper position. But those that were concerned in the murder of Agis, perceiving the design, and fearing that upon Archidamus's return that they should be **called to an account**, received him on his coming privately into town, and joined in bringing him home, and presently after murdered him.

Whether Cleomenes was against it, as Phylarchus thinks, or whether he was persuaded by his friends, or let him (Archidamus) fall into their hands, is uncertain; however, they were most blamed, as having forced his consent. He, still resolving to remodel the state, bribed the ephors to send him out to war; and won the affections of many others by means of his mother Cratesiclea, who spared no cost and was very zealous to promote her son's ambition; and though of herself she had no inclination to marry, yet for his sake she accepted, as her husband, one of the chiefest citizens for wealth and power.

Part Three

So Cleomenes leading his army into the field, won a place within the territory of Megalopolis, called **Leuctra**. The Achaeans also quickly came to their aid, led by Aratus: they straight fought a battle by the city itself, where Cleomenes had the worst on the one side of his army. Howbeit Aratus would not suffer the Achaeans to follow them, because of bogs and quagmires, but sounded the retreat. But **Lydiadas**, a Megalopolitan, being angry withal, caused the horsemen he had about him to follow the chase, who pursued so fiercely, that they came amongst vines, walls, and ditches, where he was driven to disperse his men, and yet could not get out.

Cleomenes perceiving it, sent some light horsemen of the **Tarentines** and **Cretans** against him: by whom Lydiadas, valiantly fighting, was slain. Then the Lacedaemonians, being courageous for this victory, came with great cries; and giving a fierce charge upon the Achaeans, overthrew their whole army, and slew a marvellous number of them. But yet Cleomenes, at their request, suffered them to take up the dead bodies of their men to bury them. For Lydiadas's corpse, he caused it to be brought unto him, and putting a purple robe upon it, and a crown on his head, sent it in this array unto the very gates of the city of **Megalopolis** *[omission]*.

Part Four

Cleomenes was very much elated by this success, and was persuaded that if matters were wholly at his disposal he should soon overcome the Achaeans. He persuaded **Megistonus**, his mother's husband, that it was necessary to take away the authority of the ephors, and to make division of the lands among the Spartans: thus Sparta, being restored to its old equality, might aspire again to the command of all Greece. Megistonus liked the design, and engaged two or three more of his friends *[omission for length]*.

And carrying with him those whom he thought would be most against his project, Cleomenes took **Heraea** and **Asea**, two towns in league with the Achaeans, **furnished Orchomenus with provisions**, encamped before **Mantinea**, and with long marches up and down **so harassed the Lacedaemonians** that many of them, at their own request, were left behind in Arcadia, while he with the mercenaries went on toward Sparta; and by the way communicated his design to those whom he thought fitted for his purpose; and marched slowly, that he might catch the ephors at supper.

When he came near unto the city, he sent Eurycleides before, into the hall of the ephors, as though he brought them news out of the camp from him. After him, he sent also Thericion and Phoebis, and two others that had been brought up with him *[omission]*, taking with them a few soldiers.

Now whilst Eurycleides was talking with the ephors, they also came in upon them with the swords drawn, and did set upon the ephors. **Agesilaus (#2)** was hurt first of all, and falling down, made as though he had been slain, but by little and little he crept out of the hall, and got secretly into a chapel consecrated unto Fear, which was normally kept shut, but then by chance was left open: when he was come in, he shut the door fast to him. The other four of the ephors were slain presently, and above ten more besides, which came to defend them. Furthermore, for them that sat still and stirred not, they killed not a man of them, neither did keep any man that was desirous to go out of the city: but moreover, they pardoned Agesilaus, who came the next morning out of the Chapel of Fear.

Amongst the Lacedaemonians in the city of Sparta, there are not only temples of Fear and Death, but also of Laughter, and of many other such passions of the mind. They do worship Fear, not as other spirits and devils that are hurtful: but because they are persuaded that nothing preserves a commonwealth better than fear. Therefore the ephors (Aristotle is my author), when they entered upon their government, made proclamation to the people, that they should shave their mustaches and be obedient to the laws, that the laws might not be hard upon them; making, I suppose, this trivial injunction to accustom their youth to obedience even in the smallest matters. And the ancients, I think, did not imagine bravery to be plain fearlessness, but a cautious fear of blame and disgrace. For those that show most timidity towards the laws are most bold against their enemies; and those are least afraid of any danger who are most afraid of a just reproach.

[omission for length]

Narration and Discussion

"Nevertheless, Cleomenes holding still his first determination, to alter the state of the commonwealth of Sparta, as soon as possible: he so fed the ephors with money, that he brought them to be contented that he should make war" (North's translation). Why did Cleomenes' plan for a rejuvenated city depend on his continuing to fight the Achaeans?

"Nothing preserves a commonwealth better than fear." Do you agree?

Hands-on narration: Using your model, tell one or all of these stories: Cleomenes' battles against the Achaean League; the short, unhappy reign of Archidamus; the killing of the ephors.

Creative narration: Use another creative format, such as a news broadcast or artwork, to tell one of the same stories.

Lesson Six

Introduction

The Spartans were finding their old groove again, from the education of children to the re-institution of black broth and brown bread. The Achaeans, looking on, assumed that the reforms must have been enacted by force (who would want to live like that?), and that the Spartans must be on the verge of revolt; but they were wrong.

Vocabulary

pike: a *sarissa* or long spear, used in the Macedonian phalanx formation

compulsion: force

mina: a unit of currency, measured by weight in gold or silver

looseness, wantonness: undisciplined, immoral behaviour

native jests: down-home Spartan humour

pretentious: showy, trying to impress

his designs on Greece: his plan to take over the other Greek states

a prince to be spoken to but by messengers…: This is the way the Greeks had been treated by other rulers, having to wait endlessly to be heard; but Cleomenes ran a more open-door system.

we may not use strangers so hardly after our manner: we cannot treat guests with our own severe customs

After the table was removed: At Greek dinner parties, the entire table was removed after the main courses, and replaced with another table or stand that held fruits, nuts, sweets, and wine.

People

Sphaerus the philosopher: see **Lesson Four**

Eucleidas: see introductory notes

Historic Occasions

c. 227-226 B.C.: Cleomenes began his civic reforms

227 B.C.: Accession of Eucleidas (Cleomenes' brother) as his co-ruler

Reading

Part One

The next morning Cleomenes banished, by trumpet, eighty citizens of Sparta, and overthrew all the chairs of the ephors but one only, the which he reserved for himself to sit in to give audience. Then calling the people to council, he gave them a history lesson:

> He reminded them that Lycurgus (#1) had joined the senators with the kings, and how the city had been governed a long time by them, without help of any other officers. Notwithstanding, afterwards the city having great wars with the Messenians, the kings being always employed in that war, whereby they could not attend the affairs of the commonwealth at home, did choose certain of their friends to sit in judgment in their steads to determine controversies of laws, which were called ephors, and they did govern long time as the kings' ministers, howbeit that afterwards, by little and little, they took upon them absolute government by themselves and abused that power *[omission]*...

Cleomenes continued his speech:

> And therefore, if it had been possible to have banished all these foreign plagues out of Sparta, brought from foreign nations (pleasures, pastimes, money, debts, and usuries, poverty and riches), he might then have esteemed himself the happiest king that ever was, if like a good physician he had cured

119

his country of that infection, without grief or sorrow. But in that he was constrained to begin with blood, he would follow Lycurgus's example: who being neither king nor other magistrate, but a private citizen only, taking upon him the authority of the king, boldly came into the marketplace with force and armed men, and made King Charilaus, that then reigned, so afraid that he was driven to take sanctuary in one of the temples.

But King Charilaus being a prince of a noble nature, and loving the honour of his country, took part with Lycurgus, adding to his advice and counsel for the alteration of the state of the government of the commonwealth, which he did confirm. Hereby, then, it appeareth that Lycurgus saw it was a hard thing to alter the commonwealth without force and fear: in the use of which he himself, he said, had been so moderate as to do no more than put out of the way those who opposed themselves to Sparta's happiness and safety.

For the rest of the nation, the whole land was now their common property; debtors should be cleared of their debts, and examination made of those who were not citizens, that the bravest men might thus be made free Spartans, and give aid in arms to save the city; "and we," he said, "may no longer see Laconia, for want of men to defend it, wasted by the Aetolians and Illyrians."

Then he himself first, with his step-father, Megistonus, and his friends, gave up all their wealth into one public stock, and all the other citizens followed the example. The land was divided, and everyone that he had banished had a share assigned him [as well]; for he promised to restore all as soon as things were settled and in quiet.

Part Two

So when he had replenished the number of the citizens of Sparta, with the choicest, most honest men of their neighbours: he made four thousand footmen well-armed, and taught them to use their **pikes** with both hands, instead of their darts with one hand, and to carry their shields with a good strong handle, and not buckled with a leather thong. Afterwards he took order for the education of children, and to restore the ancient Laconian discipline again: and did all these things in manner by the help of **Sphaerus the philosopher**. Insomuch as he had quickly set up again schoolhouses for children, and also brought them to the older order of diet: and all but a very few, without **compulsion**, were willing to fall to their old institution of life. And, that the name of monarch might give them no jealousy, he made **Eucleidas**, his brother, partner in the throne; and that was the only time that Sparta had two kings of the same family.

Furthermore, understanding that the Achaeans and Aratus were of opinion that he would not venture out of Sparta and leave the city now unsettled in the midst of so great an alteration, he thought it great and serviceable to his designs to show his enemies the zeal and forwardness of his troops. And, therefore, making an incursion into the territories of Megalopolis, he wasted the country far and wide, and collected considerable spoils. And at last, taking a company of actors as they were travelling from Messene, he set up a stage within the enemy's country, offering a prize of forty **minas** for the victor; and sat a whole day to look upon them, not for the pleasure he took in the sight of it, but wishing to show his disregard for his enemies; and by a display of his contempt, to prove the extent of his superiority to them. For his alone, of all the Greek or royal armies, had no stage-players, no jugglers, no dancing or singing women attending it, but was free from all sorts of **looseness, wantonness**, and festivity; the young men being for the most part at their exercises, and the old men giving them lessons, or, at leisure times, diverting themselves with their **native jests**, and quick Laconian answers *[omission]*.

But of all these things, the king himself was their schoolmaster and example; he was a living pattern of temperance before every man's eyes; and his course of living was neither more stately, nor more expensive, nor in any way more **pretentious**, than that of his people. And this was a considerable advantage to him in **his designs on Greece**. For the Grecians having cause of suit and negotiation with other kings and princes, did not wonder so much at the pomp and riches of those kings, as they did abhor and detest their pride and insolence, so disdainfully they would answer them that had to do with them. But contrarily, when they went unto Cleomenes, who was a king in name and deed as they were, finding no purple robes nor stately mantles, nor rich embroidered beds, nor **a prince to be spoken to but by messengers, gentlemen ushers, and supplications, and yet with great ado**: and seeing him also come plainly appareled unto them, with a good countenance, and courteously answering the matters they came for: he thereby did marvellously win their hearts and goodwill, that when they returned home, they said he only was the worthy king that came of the race of Hercules.

His common everyday meal was in an ordinary room, very sparing, and after the Laconic manner; and when he entertained ambassadors, or strangers, two more couches were added, and a little better dinner provided by his servants; not with pastry and conserves, but with more store of meat, and some better wine than ordinary. For he one day reproved one of his friends, that, bidding strangers to supper, he gave them nothing but black broth, and brown bread only, according to their Laconian manner: "Nay," said he, "**we may not use strangers so hardly after our manner**."

After the table was removed, a stand was brought in, whereupon they set a bowl of copper full of wine, two silver bowls, which held about a pint apiece, and a few silver cups, of which he that pleased might drink; but wine was not urged on any of the guests. Furthermore, there was no sport, nor any pleasant song, to make the company merry, nor was any required. For Cleomenes himself would entertain them with some pretty questions, or pleasant tale: whereby, as his talk was not severe and without pleasure, so was it also pleasant without insolence. For he was of opinion, that to win men by gifts or money, as other kings and princes did, was dishonest and artificial: but to seek their goodwills by courteous means, and pleasantries, and therewith to mean good faith, was that which he thought most fit and honourable for a prince. For this was his mind, that there was no other difference betwixt a friend and a mercenary: but that the one is won with money, and the other with civility and good entertainment [*Dryden: character and conversation*].

Narration and Discussion

Why was Cleomenes able to enact the reforms (in a relatively short time) that Agis had proposed but been unable to carry out?

What do the dinner-party descriptions show about the character of Cleomenes?

Hands-on narration: Show Cleomenes in the place of the ephors, and add Eucleidas as the Eurypontid king. The model could also be used to show Cleomenes' invasion of the Megalopolitan territory.

Creative narration: Write or act out a scene between two or three Spartan women who meet at the market, discussing what's in their grocery baskets and how their children's schooling is going.

Lesson Seven

Introduction

With his increasing military success, Cleomenes began to demand more concessions from those he had defeated. When he suddenly became too ill to attend a parliament with the Achaeans, Aratus took advantage of the lull to suggest that they should ask for help (once again) from Macedon. But the Achaeans, exasperatingly, seemed to prefer the idea of being ruled by Sparta.

Vocabulary

the Hecatombaeum: a site for religious sacrifices

steer the rudder: steer the ship, take the helm

stifled: suffocated, was unable to breathe

rapacity: greed

infamous: well known, but not in a good way

consumed away: Antigonus was suffering from tuberculosis

composed: settled

with a flea in his ear: making it clear that he was unwelcome

People

Hyperbatas: general of the Achaean League from 226-225 B.C.

Antigonus: Antigonus III Doson was the king of Macedon from 229 B.C. until his death in 221 B.C.

Historic Occasions

226 B.C.: The Mantineans asked for help against the Achaean League

226 B.C.: The Spartans fought the Achaeans at Dymae

On the Map

Pherae: a city-state in Thessaly

Dymae: or Dyme; a city of Achaea, near the coast of the **Ionian Sea**

Lerna: a region south of **Argos**

Aegium: a town of Achaea

Reading

Part One

The Mantineans were the first that requested Cleomenes' aid; and when he entered their city by night, they aided him to expel the Achaean garrison, and put themselves under his protection. But he, referring them to the use and government of their own laws and liberty, departed from thence the same day, and went unto the city of Tegea. Shortly after, he compassed about Arcadia, and came unto **Pherae** in Arcadia, intending either to give the Achaeans battle, or to bring Aratus into disrepute for refusing to engage, and suffering him to waste the country. **Hyperbatas** was at that time general of the Achaeans, but Aratus did bear all the sway and authority, marching forth with their whole strength, and encamping in **Dymae**, near **the Hecatombaeum**. Cleomenes came up, and thinking it not advisable to pitch his camp between Dymae, a city of the enemies, and the camp of the Achaeans, he boldly dared the Achaeans, and forced them to a battle, overthrew them, made them flee, and slew a great number in the field, and took many of them also prisoners. Departing from thence, he went and set upon the city of Langon, and drove the garrison of the Achaeans out of it, and restored the city again unto the Eleans.

The Achaeans were then in very hard state. Aratus, who of custom was wont to be their general (or at the least once in two years), refused now to take the charge, although the Achaeans did specially pray and entreat him: the which was an ill act of him, to let another **steer the rudder** in so dangerous a storm and tempest. Cleomenes at first proposed fair and easy conditions by his ambassadors to the Achaeans; but afterwards he sent others, and required the chief command to be settled upon him; and that for all other matters he would deal reasonably with them, and presently deliver them up their towns and prisoners again, which he had taken of theirs. The Achaeans were willing to come to an agreement upon those terms, and invited Cleomenes to **Lerna**, where an assembly was to be held. But it chanced then that Cleomenes marching thither, being very hot, drank cold water, and fell of such a bleeding withal, that his voice was taken from him, and he almost **stifled**. Therefore being unable to continue his journey, he sent the chiefest of the captives to the Achaeans, and, putting off the meeting for some time, retired to Lacedaemon.

This ruined the affairs of Greece, which was just beginning in some sort to recover from its disasters, and to show some capability of delivering itself from the insolence and **rapacity** of the Macedonians. For Aratus, either for that he trusted not Cleomenes, or for that he was afraid of his power, or that he otherwise envied his honour and prosperity, to see him risen to such incredible greatness in so short a time; and thinking it also too great shame and dishonour to him, to suffer this young man in a moment to deprive him of his great honour and power which he had possessed so long time, by the space of thirty years together, ruling all Greece: first, he sought by force to terrify the

Achaeans, and to make them break off from this peace. But in fine, finding that they little regarded his threats, and that he could not prevail with them, for that they were afraid of Cleomenes' valiantness and courage, whose request they thought reasonable, for that he sought but to restore Peloponnesus into her former ancient estate again: he fell then into a practice far unhonest for a Grecian, very **infamous** for himself, but most dishonourable for the former noble acts he had done. For Aratus brought **Antigonus** into Greece, and filled the country of Peloponnesus with Macedonians, whom he himself in his youth had driven thence, when he had taken from them the castle of Corinth.

[omission for length and content]

And furthermore, fleeing them that were contented with brown bread, and with the plain coarse capes of the Lacedaemonians, and that went about to take away riches (which was the chiefest matter they did accuse Cleomenes for), and to provide for the poor: he went and put himself and all Achaea into the crown and diadem, the purple robe, and proud imperious commandments of the Macedonians, fearing lest men should think that Cleomenes could command him. Furthermore his folly was such that, having garlands of flowers on his head, he did sacrifice unto Antigonus, and sing songs in praise of his honour, as if he had been a god, where he was but a rotten man, **consumed away**.

I write this not out of any design to disgrace Aratus, for in many things he showed himself a true lover of Greece, and a great man; but to make us see the frailty and weakness of man's nature: the which, though it have never so excellent virtues, cannot yet bring forth such perfect fruit, but that it hath ever some maim and blemish.

Part Two

The Achaeans meeting again in assembly at Argos, and Cleomenes having come from Tegea, there were great hopes that all differences would be **composed**. But Aratus, Antigonus and he having already agreed upon the chief articles of their league, fearing that Cleomenes would carry all before him, and either win or force the multitude to comply with his demands, proposed that, having three hundred hostages put into his hands, he should come alone into the town, or bring his army to the place of exercise, called the Cyllarabium, outside the city, and treat there.

Then Cleomenes had heard their answer, he told them that they had done him wrong: for they should have advertised him of it before he had taken his journey, and not now when he was almost hard at their gates, to send him back again, **with a flea in his ear**. And writing a letter to the Achaeans about the same subject, the greatest part of which was an accusation of Aratus (while Aratus, on the other side, spoke violently against him to the assembly), he hastily dislodged, and sent a trumpeter to denounce war against the Achaeans: not to Argos, but to **Aegium**, as Aratus writes, that he might not give them notice enough to make provision for their defense. There had also been a movement among the Achaeans themselves, and the cities were eager for revolt; the common people expecting a division of the land, and a release from their debts, and the chief men being in many places ill-disposed to Aratus, and some of them angry and indignant with him for having brought the Macedonians into Peloponnesus.

Narration and Discussion

Cleomenes had persuaded the Spartans to resume their traditional lifestyle, including plain dress. Why did Aratus go to such extremes in the other direction?

For further thought: "I write this not out of any design to disgrace Aratus…but to make us see the frailty and weakness of man's nature: the which, though it have never so excellent virtues, cannot yet bring forth such perfect fruit, but that it hath ever some maim and blemish." Does this help to explain Plutarch's aim in writing biographies?

Hands-on narration: This would be a good time to add Macedon, and the figure of Antigonus, to the actors currently "on stage."

Creative narration: Draw a cartoon that might have appeared in either the "Spartan Times" or the "Achaean Daily Mail."

Lesson Eight

Introduction

The Spartans' rediscovered power made them enough of a threat that Aratus gave up trying to fight them; but not before sending Antigonus and his very powerful Macedonian army marching in their direction.

Vocabulary

Nemean Games: a religious and athletic event held every two years; originally held in Nemea, but they had been moved to **Argos**.

assailing: attacking

signal: significant, noteworthy

posted: raced

phalanx: a tight battle formation used by the Macedonians

the second watch of the night: between about 9:00 p.m. and midnight

the suspected: those suspected of disloyalty

relics: remains

People

Tritymallus: In his *Life of Aratus*, Plutarch calls him Tripylus.

Megistonus: Cleomenes' stepfather (see **Lesson Five**)

Historic Occasions

224 B.C.: Death of Cleomenes' wife Agiatis

On the Map

Pellene: the most easterly of the twelve Achaean cities, bordering on

Sicyon to the east. It changed hands several times during the war.

Pheneus: a town in the northeastern part of Arcadia, south of Pellene

Penteleium (Pentellium): a mountain fortress near Pheneus

Sicyon: a city-state in northern Peloponnesus; the hometown of Aratus

Cleoneae: a city between Argos and Corinth

Phlius: a city-state in northeastern Peloponnesus

Geranea: a mountain range between Peloponnesus and central Greece

Lechaeum: the port used by the city of Corinth

Heraeum: a religious site, located on a **promontory** (a point of high land) at the end of the **Perachora** peninsula

Epidaurus: a city on the **Saronic Gulf**

Reading

Part One

Encouraged by [all this], Cleomenes invaded Achaea, and first took **Pellene** by surprise, and beat out the Achaean garrison, and afterwards brought over **Pheneus** and **Penteleium** to his side.

Now the Achaeans, suspecting some treacherous designs at Corinth and **Sicyon**, sent their horse and mercenaries out of Argos, to have an eye upon those cities; and they themselves went to Argos to celebrate the **Nemean Games**. Cleomenes thought (which fell out true) that if he went to Argos, he should find the city full of people that were come to see the feasts and games; and that, **assailing** them upon the sudden, he should put them in a marvellous fear. He marched with his army to the walls, and taking the quarter of the town called Aspis, which lies above the theatre, well-fortified and hard to be approached, he so terrified them that none offered to resist, and they agreed (first) to accept a garrison, (second) to give twenty citizens for hostages, (third) to assist the Lacedaemonians, and (fourth) that he should have the chief command.

This action considerably increased his reputation and his power; for the ancient Spartan kings, though they in many ways endeavoured to effect it, could never bring Argos to be permanently theirs. And Pyrrhus, the most experienced captain, though he entered the city by force, could not keep possession, but was slain himself, with a considerable part of his army. Therefore they admired the diligence and counsel of Cleomenes. And where every man did mock him before, for imitating, as they said, Solon and Lycurgus (#1), in releasing the people from their debts, and in equalizing the property of the citizens, were now forced to admit that this was the cause of the change in the Spartans. For before they were very low in the world, and so weak and out of heart that the Aetolians, invading Laconia, brought away fifty thousand slaves; so that one of the elder Spartans is reported to have said that their enemies had done them a great pleasure, to rid their country of such a rabble of rascals; and yet a little while after, by merely recurring once again to their native customs, and re-entering the track of other ancient discipline, they were able to give, as though it had been under the eyes and conduct of Lycurgus himself, the most **signal** instances of courage and obedience, raising Sparta to her ancient place as the commanding state of Greece, and recovering all Peloponnesus.

Part Two

After Cleomenes had taken the city of Argos, the cities also of **Cleoneae** and **Phlius** did yield themselves unto him. Aratus in the meantime remained at Corinth, searching after some who were reported to favour the Spartan interest. But when news was brought to him that Argos was taken, and that he perceived also the city of Corinth did lean unto Cleomenes' part, and was willing to be rid of the Achaeans: he then calling the people to council in Corinth, secretly stole to one of the gates of the city, and causing his horse to be brought unto him, took his back, and fled to Sicyon.

When the Corinthians heard of it, they took to their horsebacks also, striving who should be there soonest, and **posted** in such haste unto Cleomenes at the city of Argos, that many of them (as Aratus writeth) killed their horses by the way; he adds that Cleomenes was very angry with the Corinthians for letting him escape; and that

Megistonus came from Cleomenes to him, desiring him to deliver up the castle of Corinth, which was then garrisoned by the Achaeans, and offered him a considerable sum of money; and that he answered that matters were not now in his power, but he in theirs. Thus Aratus himself writes.

Part Three

Now Cleomenes, departing from the city of Argos, overcame the Troezenians, the Epidaurians, and the Hermioneans. After that, he came unto Corinth, and presently entrenched the castle there round about; and sending for Aratus's friends and stewards, commanded them to keep Aratus's house and goods carefully for him, and sent **Tritymallus** the Messenian again unto Aratus, desiring that the castle might be equally garrisoned by the Spartans and Achaeans, and promising to Aratus himself double the pension that he received from King Ptolemy. But Aratus refusing it, sent his son unto Antigonus with other hostages, and persuaded the Achaeans to deliver up the castle of Corinth into Antigonus's hands.

Upon this Cleomenes invaded the territory of the Sicyonians, and by a decree of the Corinthians, accepted Aratus's estate as a gift.

Part Four

In the meantime Antigonus, with a great army, was passing **Geranea**; and Cleomenes, thinking it more advisable to fortify and garrison, not the isthmus, but the mountains called Onea, and by a war of posts and positions to weary the Macedonians, rather than to venture a set battle with the highly disciplined **phalanx**, put his design into execution, and very much distressed Antigonus. For he had not brought victuals sufficient for his army; nor was it easy to force a way through whilst Cleomenes guarded the pass. He attempted by night to pass through **Lechaeum**, but failed and lost some men; so that Cleomenes and his army were mightily encouraged, and so flushed with the victory that they went merrily to supper.

Antigonus on the other side fell into despair, to see himself brought by necessity into such hard terms. He was proposing to march to the promontory of **Heraeum**, and thence transport his army in boats to

Sicyon, which would take up a great deal of time, and require much preparation and means. But the same night there came some of Aratus's friends of the Argives, who coming from Argos by sea, brought news that the Argives were rebelled against Cleomenes. The practiser of this rebellion was one Aristoteles, and he had no hard task to persuade the common people; for they were all angry with Cleomenes for not releasing them from their debts as they expected. Accordingly, obtaining fifteen hundred of Antigonus's soldiers, Aratus sailed to **Epidaurus**; but Aristoteles, not staying for his coming, drew out the citizens, and fought against the garrison of the castle; and Timoxenus, with the Achaeans from Sicyon, came to his assistance.

Cleomenes heard the news about **the second watch of the night**. He sent for Megistonus in haste, and commanded him in anger speedily to go and set things right at Argos. Megistonus had passed his word for the Argives' loyalty, and had persuaded him not to banish **the suspected**. So sending him away forthwith with two thousand men, he himself kept watch upon Antigonus, and encouraged the Corinthians, pretending that there was no great matter in the commotions at Argos, but only a little disturbance raised by a few inconsiderable persons.

But when Megistonus, entering Argos, was slain, and the garrison could scarce hold out, and frequent messengers came to Cleomenes for succour, Cleomenes then being afraid that the enemies having taken Argos, would stop his way to return back into his country, who having opportunity safely to spoil Laconia, and also to besiege the city itself of Sparta, that had but a few men to defend it: he departed with his army from Corinth, and immediately lost that city, for Antigonus entered it, and garrisoned the town.

But when he saw Antigonus with his phalanx descending from the mountains into the plain, and the horse on all sides entering the city, he thought it impossible to maintain his post; and, gathering all his men together, he came safely down and made his retreat under the walls: having in so short a time possessed himself of great power, and in one journey, so to say, having made himself master of all Peloponnesus, and now lost all again in as short a time.

For some of his allies at once withdrew and forsook him; others also immediately after surrendered up their towns unto Antigonus. His hopes thus defeated, as he was leading back the **relics** of his forces, news came to him in the night from Lacedaemon, which grieved him as much as the loss of all his conquests: for he was advertised of the death of his wife Agiatis, whom he loved so dearly, that in the midst of his chiefest prosperity and victories, he made often journeys to Sparta to see her. It could not be but a marvellous grief unto Cleomenes, who being a young man, had lost so virtuous and fair a young lady, so dearly beloved of him: and yet he gave not place unto his sorrow, neither did grief overcome his noble courage, but he used the selfsame voice, apparel, and countenance, that he did before.

Then taking order with his private captains about his affairs, and having provided also for the safety of the Tegeans: he went the next morning by break of day unto Sparta. After he had privately lamented the sorrow of his wife's death, with his mother and children, he presently bent his mind again to public causes.

Narration and Discussion

Tell how Cleomenes "having made himself master of all Peloponnesus, now lost all again in as short a time."

Cleomenes was now at a difficult point, both personally and as the ruler and general of Sparta. What do you think would be his next move? If you could advise Cleomenes, what would you say to him?

Hands-on narration: This would be a good time to add Argos and Corinth to the states included in the model; you will also want to note the deaths of Agiatis and Megistonus.

Lesson Nine

Introduction

Sparta was not powerful enough to stand against Macedonia alone, so Cleomenes asked for help from Egypt. King Ptolemy didn't require much in return: only Cleomenes' mother and son as hostages. At the same time, the Macedonians were attacking the borders of Spartan territory. It seemed that all would be lost; but "then there fell into his mind a marvellous great enterprise, unlooked for of every man."

Vocabulary

in pledge: as hostages

composed her countenance: got hold of herself

expedient: good, beneficial

adversity: trials, trouble

making such of the helots as could pay…: The helots were the lowest class in ancient Sparta, similar to serfs. By encouraging them to buy freedom, Cleomenes raised enough money to outfit his army.

victual themselves: take what food they would need

plundered: robbed, looted

mantle: cloak

People

Philopoemen (253-183 B.C.): Philopoemen was a leader of the Achaean League and the subject of one of Plutarch's *Lives*.

Ptolemy (#1): Ptolemy III Euergetes is also referred to as the "old" King Ptolemy, as he died soon after Cleomenes' arrival in 222 B.C.

Panteus: a friend of Cleomenes

Historic Occasions

227/226 B.C.: Cleomenes' mother and son were sent to Egypt

222 B.C.: Cleomenes seized Megalopolis

On the Map

Taenarus: the southernmost point of mainland Greece

Sellasia: a village 6.2 miles (10 km) north of Sparta

Rhoeteum: or Rhoiteion; not the Greek city in **Anatolia**, but one by the same name in the territory of Megalopolis

Reading

Part One

Now Cleomenes had sent unto **Ptolemy (#1)**, the king of Egypt, who had promised him aid, but upon demand to have his mother and children **in pledge**. So he was a long time before he would for shame make his mother privy unto it, and went oftentimes of purpose to let her understand it: but when he first came, he had not the heart to break it to her. She first suspecting a thing, asked Cleomenes' friends, if her son had not somewhat to say unto her, that he dared not utter. At last, Cleomenes venturing to tell her, she fell a-laughing, and told him,

> "Why, how cometh it to pass, that thou hast kept it
> thus long, and wouldst not tell me? Come, come,"
> said she, "put me straight into a ship, and send me
> whither thou wilt, that this body of mine may do
> some good unto my country, before crooked age
> consumes my life without profit."

Then all things being prepared for the journey, they went by land, accompanied with the army, to **Taenarus**. Where, Cratesiclea being ready to embark, she took Cleomenes aside into the Temple of Neptune, and embracing and kissing him, perceiving that his heart yearned for sorrow of her departure, she said unto him:

> "O King of Lacedaemon, let no man see for shame,
> when we come out of the temple, that we have wept
> and dishonoured Sparta. For that only is in our
> power, and for the rest, as it pleaseth the gods, so let
> it be."

When she had spoken these words, and **composed her countenance**: she went then to take her ship, with a little son of Cleomenes, and commanded the master of the ship to hoist sail.

Now when she was arrived in Egypt, and understood that Ptolemy received ambassadors from Antigonus, and were in talk to make peace with him: and hearing also that Cleomenes though the Achaeans invited and urged him to an agreement, was afraid, for her sake, to come to any, without Ptolemy's consent; she wrote unto him, that he should not spare to do anything that should be **expedient** for the honour of Sparta, without fear of displeasing Ptolemy, or for regards of an old woman and a young boy. Such was the noble mind of this worthy lady in her son Cleomenes' **adversity**.

Part Two

Furthermore, Antigonus having taken the city of Tegea, and sacked the other cities of Orchomenum, and Mantinea: Cleomenes was shut up within the narrow bounds of Laconia; and **making such of the helots as could pay five Attic pounds free of Sparta**; and, by that means, getting together five hundred talents, and arming two thousand after the Macedonian fashion, that he might make a body fit to oppose Antigonus's "White Shields," there fell into his mind a marvellous great enterprise, unlooked for of every man.

The city of **Megalopolis** was at that time as great as Sparta. It had the forces of the Achaeans and of Antigonus encamping beside it; and it was chiefly the Megalopolitans' doing that Antigonus had been called in to assist the Achaeans. Cleomenes, resolving to snatch the city (no other word so well suits so rapid and so surprising an action), commanded his soldiers to **victual themselves** for five days, and marched to **Sellasia**, as though he had meant to have ravaged the country of the Argives; but from thence making a descent into the territories of Megalopolis, and refreshing his army about **Rhoeteum**, he suddenly took the road by Helicus, and advanced directly upon the city. When he was not far off the town, he sent **Panteus**, with two regiments, to surprise a portion of the wall between two towers, which he learnt to be the most unguarded quarter of the Megalopolitans' fortifications; and with the rest of his forces he followed leisurely. When Panteus came thither, finding not only that place of the wall without guard or watch which Cleomenes had told him of, but also the most part of that side without defense: he took some part of the wall at his first coming, and manned it, and overthrew another piece of it also, putting them all to the sword that did defend it.

Whilst he was thus busied, Cleomenes came up to him, and was got with his army within the city, before the Megalopolitans knew of the surprise. When, after some time, they learned their misfortune, some left the town immediately, taking with them what property they could; others armed and engaged the enemy; and though they were not able to beat them out, yet they gave their citizens time and opportunity safely to retire, so that there were not above one thousand persons taken in the town, all the rest flying, with their wives and children, and escaping to Messene.

The greatest number, also, of those that armed and fought the enemy were saved, and very few taken, amongst whom were Lysandridas and Thearidas, two men of great power and reputation amongst the Megalopolitans; and therefore the soldiers, as soon as they were taken, brought them to Cleomenes. And Lysandridas, when he saw Cleomenes a good way off, cried out aloud unto him: "O King of Lacedaemon, this day thou hast an occasion offered thee to do a more famous princely act, than that which thou hast already done, and that will make thy name also more glorious."

Cleomenes musing what he would request: "Well," quoth he, "what is that thou requirest? One thing I will tell thee beforehand, thou shalt not make me restore your city to you again."

"Yet," quoth Lysandridas, "let me request thus much then, that ye do not destroy it, but rather replenish it with friends and confederates, which hereafter will be true and faithful to you: and that shall you do, giving the Megalopolitans their city again, and preserving such a number of people as have forsaken it."

Cleomenes pausing awhile, answered that it was a hard thing to believe that. "But yet," quoth he, "let honour take place with us, before profit." Having said this, he sent the two men to Messene with a herald from himself, offering the Megalopolitans their city again, if they would forsake the Achaean interest, and be on his side.

But though Cleomenes made these generous and humane proposals, **Philopoemen** would not suffer them to break their league with the Achaeans; and accusing Cleomenes to the people, as if his design was not to restore the city, but to take the citizens too, he forced Thearidas and Lysander to leave Messene. (This was that Philopoemen who was afterwards chief of the Achaeans and a man of the greatest reputation amongst the Greeks, as I have related it in his own *Life*.)

This news coming to Cleomenes, though he had before taken strict care that the city should not be **plundered**, yet then, being in anger, and out of all patience, he despoiled the place of all the valuables, and sent the statues and the pictures to Sparta; and demolished a great part of the city. He then marched away for fear of Antigonus and the Achaeans; but they never stirred, for they were at Aegium, at a council of war. There Aratus mounted the speaker's place, and wept a long while, holding his **mantle** before his face; and at last, the company being amazed, and commanding him to speak, he said, "Megalopolis is destroyed by Cleomenes." The assembly instantly dissolved, the Achaeans being astounded at the suddenness and greatness of the loss; and Antigonus, intending to send speedy succours, when he found his forces gather very slowly out of their winter quarters, sent them orders to continue there still; and he himself marched to Argos with a small body of men.

Narration and Discussion

Was the plan to capture Megalopolis a good one? Why was it unsuccessful? Where might this leave the Spartans?

Cleomenes said to Lysandrides, "Let honour take place with us, before profit." Dryden translates it, "With us let profit always yield to glory." What did Cleomenes mean?

Hands-on narration: Add Egypt and King Ptolemy to the model.

Lesson Ten

Introduction

In the summer of 222 B.C., the Spartans fought one last time against the combined armies of the Achaean League and the Macedonians. Their defeat was not obvious from the start, although the Spartans were outnumbered (something that didn't usually deter them). If Cleomenes had been able to hold out just a bit longer, Plutarch says, things might have ended differently; but the difference in numbers, a lack of money, and an act of treason combined to spell disaster.

Vocabulary

deliberation: serious thought

hazard: risk

railed at: criticized

wanton scorn: utter contempt

scornful pleasantry: mockery, ridicule

devastations: destruction, damage

in this conjecture: in this coming together of events

unto all posterity: to future generations

People

Polybius: a historian, one of Plutarch's sources

Historic Occasions

Summer of 222 B.C.: Spartan defeat at the **Battle of Sellasia** marked the end of the Cleomenean War

On the Map

Oligyrtus: a fortress, and also the mountain on which it was situated

harbour of Gythium: or Gytheio; the seaport closest to Sparta

Reading

Part One

And now the second enterprise of Cleomenes, though it had the look of a desperate and frantic adventure, yet in **Polybius's** opinion, was done with mature **deliberation** and great foresight. For knowing very well that the Macedonians were dispersed into their winter quarters, and that Antigonus with his friends and a few mercenaries about him wintered in Argos: upon these considerations (Cleomenes) invaded the country of the Argives, hoping to shame Antigonus to a battle upon unequal terms, or else if he did not dare to fight, to bring him into disrepute with the Achaeans. And this accordingly happened. For Cleomenes wasting, plundering, and spoiling the whole country, the Argives, in grief and anger at the loss, gathered in crowds at the king's gates, crying out that he should either fight, or surrender his command to better and braver men.

But Antigonus, as became an experienced captain, accounting it rather dishonourable foolishly to **hazard** his army and quit his security, than merely to be **railed at** by other people, would not march out against Cleomenes, but stood firm to his convictions. Cleomenes, in the meantime, brought his army up to the very walls; and having without opposition spoiled the country, and insulted over his enemies, drew off again.

A little while after, being informed that Antigonus designed a new advance to Tegea, and thence to invade Laconia, Cleomenes rapidly took his soldiers, and marching by a side-road, appeared early in the morning before Argos, and wasted the fields about it. The corn he did not cut down, as is usual, with reaping-hooks and knives, but beat it down with great wooden staves made like broadswords, as if, in mere contempt and **wanton scorn**, while travelling on his way, without any effort or trouble, he spoiled and destroyed their harvest. But when they came to the exercise ground called Cyllabaris, certain of the soldiers going about to have set it afire, Cleomenes would not suffer them, and told them that the mischief he had done at Megalopolis was rather angrily than honestly done.

And when Antigonus, first of all, came hastily back to Argos, and then occupied the mountains and passes with his posts, he (Cleomenes) professed to disregard and despise it all; and sent heralds to him to desire the keys of the Temple of Juno, as if after he had done sacrifice, he would depart his way. And with this **scornful pleasantry** upon Antigonus, having sacrificed to the goddess under the walls of the temple, which was shut, he went to Phlius; and from thence driving out those that garrisoned **Oligyrtus**, he marched down to Orchomenus.

These enterprises not only encouraged the citizens, but made him appear to the very enemies to be a man worthy of high command, and capable of great things. For every man judged him to be a skillful soldier, and a valiant captain, that with the power of one only city, he did maintain war against the kingdom of Macedon, against all the people of Peloponnesus, and against the treasure of so great a king: and withal, not only to keep his own country of Laconia from being spoiled, but far otherwise to hurt his enemies' countries, and to take so many great cities of theirs *[omission]*.

Part Two

King Antigonus, coming to the war with great resources to spend, wore out Cleomenes, whose poverty made it difficult for him to provide the merest sufficiency of pay for the mercenaries, or of provisions for the citizens. For, in all other respects, time favoured Cleomenes; for Antigonus's affairs at home began to be disturbed. For the barbarians wasted and overran Macedonia while he was absent, and at that particular time a vast army of Illyrians had entered the country; to be freed from whose **devastations**, the Macedonians sent for Antigonus. If these letters had been brought to him but a little before the battle, Antigonus would have gone his way, and left the Achaeans.

But Fortune, that loves to determine the greatest affairs by a minute, **in this conjecture** showed such an exact niceness of time, that immediately after the Battle of Sellasia was over, and Cleomenes had lost his army and his city, the messengers came up and called for Antigonus; the which made the overthrow of King Cleomenes so much more lamentable. For if he had delayed battle but two days longer, when the Macedonians had been gone, he might have made what peace he would with the Achaeans: but for lack of money, he was driven (as Polybius writeth) to give battle with twenty thousand men against thirty thousand. And approving himself an admirable commander in this difficulty, his citizens showing an extraordinary courage, and his mercenaries bravery enough, he was overborne by the different way of fighting, and the weight of the heavy-armed phalanx.

Phylarchus also affirms that the treachery of some about him was the chief cause of Cleomenes' ruin. For Antigonus gave orders that the Illyrians and Acarnanians should march round by a secret way, and encompass the other wing, which Eucleidas, Cleomenes' brother, commanded; and then drew out the rest of his forces to the battle. And Cleomenes, from a convenient rising, viewing his order, and not seeing any of the Illyrians and Acarnanians, began to suspect that Antigonus had sent them upon some such design; and calling for Damoteles, who was at the head of those specially appointed to such ambush duty, he bade him carefully to look after and discover the enemy's designs upon the rear. Damoteles, that was bribed before (as it is reported) with money, told him that all was clear in the rearward, and bade him look to overthrow his enemies before him.

Cleomenes trusting this report, set forward against Antigonus, and in the end, his citizens of Sparta which he had about him gave such a fierce charge upon the squadron of the Macedonian footmen, that they drove them back about half a mile off. But then making a stand, and seeing the danger which the surrounding wing, commanded by his brother Eucleidas, was in, he cried out aloud: "Alas, good brother, thou art but slain, yet thou diest valiantly, and honestly, and thy death shall be a worthy example **unto all posterity**, and shall be sung by the praises of the women of Sparta."

So Eucleidas and his men being slain, the enemies came straight to set upon Cleomenes' wing. Cleomenes then seeing his men discouraged, and that they dared no longer resist the enemy, fled, and saved himself. Many of the mercenary soldiers also were slain at this battle; and of six thousand Spartans, there were left alive but only two hundred.

Part Three

Now Cleomenes being returned unto Sparta, the citizens coming to see him, he gave them counsel to yield themselves unto Antigonus the conqueror; and for himself, if either alive or dead he could do anything for the honour and benefit of Sparta, that he would willingly do it. The women of the city also, coming unto them that fleeing had escaped with him, when he saw them unarm the men, and bring them drink to refresh them with; he also went home to his own house.

Then a maid of the house *[omission]* came unto him as her manner was, to refresh him coming hot from the battle: howbeit he would not drink though he was extreme dry, nor sit being very weary, but armed as he was, laid his arm across upon a pillar, and leaning his head upon it, reposed himself a little, and casting in his mind all the ways that were to be thought of; and then with his friends set out at once for the **harbour of Gythium**, and there having his ships which he had appointed for the purpose, he hoisted sail, and departed his way.

Immediately after his departure, came Antigonus into the city of Sparta, and treated courteously the citizens and inhabitants he found, and did offend no man, nor proudly despise the ancient honour and dignity of Sparta, but referring them to their own laws and government. When he had sacrificed to the gods for his victory, he departed from thence the third day. For he heard that there was a great war in Macedonia, and that the country was devastated by the barbarians.

[Antigonus died shortly after this.]

Narration and Discussion

Plutarch says that Cleomenes had ships ready to sail him away in the harbour. Had he perhaps foreseen a possible loss in this battle?

Hands-on narration: Use the figures/model to show the events around the Battle of Sellasia, and its aftermath (the departure of Cleomenes and the arrival of Antigonus).

Creative narration: Antigonus appears to have been an unexpectedly gracious victor over the Spartans. Cover these events as a Spartan news reporter (or a news team, if you have a group). You may want to interview Spartan citizens, or Antigonus himself.

Lesson Eleven

Introduction

After losing his kingdom at the Battle of Sellasia, Cleomenes escaped to Egypt, where he hoped to find protection, and possibly some support for the Spartan cause.

Vocabulary

presentest: closest, nearest

vaunt: boast

list: choose

no special good: no great welcome

pension: allowance of money

had received a full dispatch: had been settled

privy council: private advisors

acquainted him with the design of taking off his brother: told him he planned to kill Magas

they were not secure of the mercenaries: King Ptolemy, apparently, was worried about being killed by the mercenary soldiers

People

Ptolemy IV Philopator (#2): the king who mistrusted Cleomenes (and who was responsible for the deaths of his own mother Berenice and brother Magas)

Sosibius: Ptolemy's chief minister

Historic Occasions

222 B.C.: Cleomenes escaped to Egypt

On the Map

Cythera: an island of Greece, and the town by the same name

Cyrene: a Greek colony in **Libya** (in northern Africa)

Alexandria: a large city in Egypt, founded by Alexander the Great

Reading

Part One

Now Cleomenes, sailing from **Cythera**, went and cast anchor in another island, called Aegialia. Then determining to sail over to the city of **Cyrene**, Therycion, one of Cleomenes' friends (a man that in wars showed himself very valiant, but a boaster beside of his own doings) took Cleomenes aside, and said thus unto him:

> "Truly O King, we have lost an honourable occasion to die in battle, though every man hath heard us **vaunt** and say that Antigonus should never overcome the king of Sparta alive, but dead. A second occasion yet is offered us to die, with much less honour and fame notwithstanding, than the first. Whither do we sail to no purpose? Why do we flee the death at hand, and seek it so far off?...let us save ourselves unto Antigonus, who in likelihood will better use us than Ptolemy, because the Macedonians are far more noble persons than the Egyptians. And if we disdain to be commanded by them which have overcome us in battle, why then will we make him lord of us, that hath not overcome us: instead of one, to make us inferior unto both, fleeing Antigonus, and serving King Ptolemy? Can we say that we go into Egypt, in respect to see your mother there? A joyful sight no doubt, when she shall show King Ptolemy's wives her son, that before was a king, a prisoner, and fugitive now. Were it not better for us, that having yet Laconia our country in sight, and our swords besides in our own hands, to deliver us from this great misery, and clear ourselves to those who at Sellasia died for the honour and defense of Sparta? Or, shall we sit lazily in Egypt, inquiring what news from Sparta, and

145

whom Antigonus hath been pleased to make governor of Lacedaemon?"

Therycion ending his oration, Cleomenes answered him thus:

"Dost thou think it a glory for thee to seek death, which is the easiest matter, and the **presentest** unto any man, that can be? And yet, wretch that thou art, thou fleest now more cowardly and shamefully than from the battle. For divers valiant men, and far better than ourselves, have often yielded unto their enemies, either by some misfortune, or compelled by greater number and multitude of men: but he, say I, that submitteth himself unto pain and misery because of the reproach and praise of men, he cannot but confess that he is overcome by his own unhappiness. For, when a man will willingly kill himself, he must not do it to be rid of pains and labour, but it must have an honourable respect and action. For, to live or die for his own respect, that cannot but be dishonourable: the which now thou persuadest me unto, to make me flee this present misery we are in, without any honour or profit in our death. And therefore, I am of opinion, that we should not yet cast off the hope we have to serve our country in time to come: but when all hope faileth us, then we may easily make ourselves away when we **list**."

Thereunto Therycion gave no answer; but as soon as he found opportunity to slip from Cleomenes, he went to the seaside, and slew himself.

Part Two

Cleomenes hoisting sail from Aegialia, landed in **Libya**, and was brought by the king's servants unto the city of **Alexandria**. King Ptolemy (#1), at his first coming, gave Cleomenes **no special good**, but indifferent entertainment. But when, upon trial, he found him a man of deep sense and great reason, and that his plain Laconic way of conversation carried with it a noble and becoming grace, that he did nothing unbecoming his birth, nor bent under fortune, and was evidently a more faithful counsellor than those who made it their business to please and flatter, he was ashamed, and repented that he had neglected so great a man, and suffered Antigonus to get so much power and reputation by ruining him. Then he began to comfort Cleomenes, and doing him as great honour as could be, promised that he would send him with ships and money into Greece, and put him again into his kingdom: and further, gave him an annual **pension** in the meantime, of four-and-twenty talents, with the which he simply and soberly entertained himself and his men about him: and bestowed all the rest in assisting his countrymen that came out of Greece into Egypt.

Part Three

But the elder Ptolemy died before Cleomenes' affairs **had received a full dispatch**. His successor, **Ptolemy IV Philopator** (#2), was *[omission]* so given over to women and wine that when he was most sober, and in his best wits, he most disposed himself to make feasts and sacrifices *[omission]*, and to gather people together, like a stage player or juggler, whilst his women did rule all the affairs of the state *[omission]*.

But when he came to be king, it appeared he had need of Cleomenes: because he was afraid of his brother Magas, who by his mother's means, was very well esteemed of among the soldiers. Wherefore he called Cleomenes to him, and made him one of his **privy council**, and **acquainted him with the design of taking off his brother**. All other of his friends did counsel him to do it; but Cleomenes only vehemently dissuaded him from it, and told him, that if it were possible, rather more brethren should be begotten unto the king for the safety of his person, and for dividing of the affairs of the kingdom between them.

And **Sosibius**, the king's greatest favourite, replying that **they were not secure of the mercenaries** whilst Magas was alive, Cleomenes returned that he need not trouble himself about that matter; for amongst the mercenaries there were above three thousand Peloponnesians, which he knew, at the twinkling of an eye, would be at his commandment to come with their armour and weapons where he would appoint them. These words of Cleomenes at that time showed his faith and the good will he bore unto the king, and the force he was of besides.

But afterwards, Ptolemy's fearfulness increasing his mistrust (as it commonly happeneth, that they that lack wit, think it the best safety to be fearful of every wagging of a straw, and to mistrust every man), the remembrance of Cleomenes' words made him much suspected of the courtiers, understanding that he had too much interest with the mercenaries; and many had this saying in their mouths, that he was a lion amidst a flock of sheep. For, in fact, such he seemed to be in the court, quietly watching and keeping his eye upon all that went on.

Narration and Discussion

Why did Therycion think it would be better to face Antigonus, rather than flee to Egypt? What was Cleomenes' response?

How were Cleomenes' words to Sosibius misinterpreted? Are there any lessons to be learned from this?

Hands-on narration: These final lessons take place in Alexandria, Egypt. Figures such as Ptolemy, Sosibius, and Magas can be added.

Creative narration: Write a letter home from one of Cleomenes' friends, describing the sudden change in Egypt.

Lesson Twelve

Introduction

Cleomenes expected that his safety in Egypt would continue, but he soon became the victim of a conspiracy. By the time he realized his own danger, escape seemed unlikely.

Vocabulary

entertained among ladies…: busy with parties

maliced: hated

but not suffered to go out again: he was placed under house arrest

discoursing: conversing, chatting

took up: scolded

he issued forth: he went out the gate

provided in the same manner: also holding swords

baffled: stymied, frustrated

People

Ptolemy (#3) the son of Chrysermus: another Ptolemy

Ptolemy (#4): yet another Ptolemy, the governor of Alexandria

Historic Occasions

219 B.C.: Death of Cleomenes

On the Map

Canopus: or Canobus; a town in the Nile Delta

Reading

Part One

He therefore gave up all thought of asking for ships and soldiers from the king. But receiving news that Antigonus was dead, that the Achaeans were engaged in a war with the Aetolians, and that the affairs of Peloponnesus, being now in very great distraction and disorder, required and invited his assistance, he desired leave to depart only with his friends; but could not obtain that, the king not so much as hearing his petition, because he was continually **entertained among ladies, with banquets, dancing, and masques**.

But Sosibius, that ruled all the realm, thought that to keep Cleomenes against his will were a hard thing, and also dangerous: and to let him go also, knowing that he was a valiant man, and of a stirring mind, and one that knew the vices and imperfections of their government: he thought that also no safe way, since no gifts nor presents that could be offered him, could soften him *[omission]*.

Now Cleomenes standing in these terms, there arrived in Alexandria one Nicagoras, a Messenian, who **maliced** Cleomenes in his heart, but pretended to be his friend. This Nicagoras on a time had sold Cleomenes certain land, but was not paid for it, either because he had no present money, or else by occasion of the wars which gave him no leisure to make payment. Cleomenes, one day by chance walking upon the sands, he saw Nicagoras landing out of his ship, being newly arrived, and knowing him, he courteously welcomed him, and asked what wind had brought him into Egypt. Nicagoras gently saluting him again, told him that he had brought King Ptolemy (#2) excellent horses of service. Cleomenes smiling, told him, "Thou hadst been better have brought him some [dancers and people to amuse him, *my paraphrase*], for they would have pleased the king better." Nicagoras faintly laughed at his answer; but within a few days after he did put him in remembrance of the land he sold him, and desired his money, protesting that he would not have troubled him if his merchandise had turned out as profitable as he had thought it would. Cleomenes answered him, that he had nothing left of all that had been given him. Nicagoras, being offended with this answer, went and told Sosibius of the mock Cleomenes gave the king. Sosibius was glad of this occasion, but yet desiring further matter to make the king offended with Cleomenes, he persuaded Nicagoras to write a letter to the king against Cleomenes, as though he had conspired to take the city of Cyrene, if the king had given him ships, money, and men of war. When Nicagoras had written this letter, he took ship, and hoisted sail. Four days after his departure, Sosibius brought his letter to the king, as though he had but newly received it; and excited the young man's fear and anger; upon which it was agreed that Cleomenes should be invited into a large house, and treated as formerly, **but not suffered to go out again**.

Part Two

This grieved Cleomenes much, but yet he was worse afraid of that which was to come, by this occasion: Ptolemy the son of Chrysermus (#3), one of the king's familiars, who had oftentimes before been very conversant and familiar with Cleomenes, and did frankly talk together in all matters: Cleomenes one day sent for him, to pray him to come unto him. Ptolemy (#3) came at his request, and familiarly **discoursing** together, went about to dissuade him from all the suspicions he had, and excused the king also for that which he had done unto him: so taking his leave he left him, not thinking that Cleomenes followed him (as he did) to the gate, where he sharply **took up** the soldiers, saying, that they were very negligent and careless in looking to "such a fearful beast as he was," and so ill to be taken, if he once escaped their hands. Cleomenes heard what he said, and went into his lodging again, Ptolemy knowing nothing that he was behind him: and Cleomenes reported the very words again unto his friends.

Then all the Spartans converting their good hope into anger, determined to be revenged of the injury Ptolemy had done them, and to die like noble Spartans, and not stay till, like fatted sacrifices, they were butchered [omission].

Part Three

They being fully resolved hereof, as you have heard: King Ptolemy (#2) by chance went unto the city of **Canopus**, and first they gave out in Alexandria, that the king minded to set Cleomenes at liberty. Then Cleomenes' friends observing the custom of the kings of Egypt, when they meant to set a prisoner at liberty (which was to send the prisoners meat and presents) did sent unto him such manner of presents, and so deceived the soldiers that had the keeping of him, saying that they brought those presents from the king. For Cleomenes himself did sacrifice unto the gods, and sent unto the soldiers that kept him, part of those presents that were sent unto him; and supping with his friends that night, made merry with them, every man being crowned with garlands [omission].

As soon as it was full moon, and all the keepers sleeping off their wine, he put on his coat, and opening his seam to bare his right shoulder, with his drawn sword in his hand, **he issued forth**, together with his friends **provided in the same manner**, making thirteen in all.

Amongst them there was one called Hippitas, who being lame, followed the first onset very well, but when he presently perceived that they were more slow in their advances for his sake, he prayed them to kill him, because they should not hinder their enterprise for him *[omission]*. By chance an Alexandrian was then riding by the door; him they threw off, and setting Hippitas on horseback, ran through the streets and cried to the people, "Liberty, liberty."

Now the people had no other courage in them, but only commended Cleomenes, and wondered at his valiantness: but otherwise to follow him, or to further his enterprise, not a man of them had any heart in them. Thus running up and down the town, they met with Ptolemy (#3) Chrysermus as he came out of the court: whereupon three of them setting on him, slew him presently. There was also another **Ptolemy (#4)** that was governor and lieutenant of the city of Alexandria: who hearing a rumour of this stir, came unto him in his coach. They went and met him, and first having driven away his guard and soldiers that went before him, they plucked him out of his coach, and slew him also.

After that they went towards the castle, with intent to set all the prisoners there at liberty to take their part; but the keepers were too quick for them, and secured the passages. Being **baffled** in this attempt, Cleomenes with his company roamed about the city, none joining with him, but all retreating from and fleeing his approach. Therefore, despairing of success, he said to his friends, "It is no marvel that women command such a cowardly people, that flee in this sort from their liberty." Thereupon he prayed them all to die like men, and like those that were brought up with him, and that were worthy of the fame of his so noble deeds.

Then the first man that made himself be slain was Hippitas, who died of a wound one of the young men of his company gave him with a sword, at his request. After him every man slew themselves, one after another, without any fear at all, saving Panteus, the same who first surprised Megalopolis. He was a fair young man, and had been very well brought up in the Laconian discipline, and better than any man of his years. Cleomenes did love him dearly, and commanded him that when he should see he were dead, and all the rest also, that then he should kill himself last of all. Panteus walked over them as they lay, and pricked every one with his dagger, to try whether any was alive; when he pricked Cleomenes on the heel amongst others, and saw that *[omission]* he was dead, he also slew himself, and fell upon him. Thus Cleomenes having reigned as king of Sparta sixteen years, being the same manner of man we have described him to be: he ended his days in this sort as ye hear.

[omission for length and content]

Narration and Discussion

What outcome did Cleomenes and his companions expect from their attempted rebellion? What seems to have finally discouraged them and caused them to take their own lives?

Hands-on narration: Although the final scenes take place in Egypt, events elsewhere, such as the death of Antigonus, can also be shown on the model.

Examination Questions

For younger students:

1. How did Cleomenes inspire the Spartans to re-embrace their old laws and lifestyle? Give two instances.

2. What are some characteristics of heroes? Would you call either Agis or Cleomenes a hero?

For older students:

1. See #2, above.

2. (High school) How and why did Agis set about the reformation of the City of Sparta?

Alternative creative examination (for any age): Design a book cover for the life of Agis or Cleomenes.

Tiberius and Gaius Gracchus

(Second Century B.C.)

The World of the Gracchi

The Gracchi brothers, Tiberius and Gaius, were born in a time of political, economic, and social upheaval in Rome, not unlike the later Industrial Revolution in Europe. During recent wars, much of Italy's farmland had been devastated. Men from rural areas were conscripted for faraway military service, and many of them never returned. The family members left were no longer able to maintain even their small farms, and they moved in large numbers to the cities, particularly Rome, hoping to make some kind of living there. With many newly wealthy (and lazy) urbanites as potential employers or customers, finding success in the city wasn't an impossible idea, but as so many people flooded in, not everyone did well, and living conditions were often wretched. Another disadvantage of this trend (at least for Rome) was that non-land-owners were disqualified for army service.

Ignoring the law that restricted the size of farms, sharp Roman businessmen bought out or out-rented the struggling farmers (see Lesson Three), and consolidated the small plots of land into big commercial operations, with slaves doing most of the work. (There were more slaves than ever now because of Roman military victories, and although this had its benefits, there was a real fear that one day the slaves would revolt.) Some of the land being bought up was *ager publicus*, or common land, which was never intended to be held privately. A lot of money was also changing hands through government contracts; a number of people were becoming very wealthy by supplying the army with weapons or tents, by running construction companies or mines, and by collecting certain types of taxes and rents that came with those contracts. You may recognize the term "publican" from the Bible, and that was the name for these contractors: *publicani*. Plutarch refers to them as simply the "wealthy men," those who were more interested in protecting their contracts and their money than in social justice.

What was an aedile, a quaestor, a consul?

The elected positions or magistracies in Rome were (starting at the bottom): quaestor, aedile, praetor, and consul. (The office of non-military tribune, or tribune of the people, was a separate position.) Ex-consuls could become censors, and a consul could become dictator if the need (usually a great emergency) arose.

Who were the tribunes?

The duty of a non-military **tribune** (sometimes called a tribune of the **plebeians**, or a "tribune of the people") was to protect the liberties of the common people from any individual or group (such as the nobles) who might take advantage of them or suppress their rights. This position was not part of the junior-senior ranking of **magistrates** such as **quaestor** and **consul**; it was an office voted on by the common people (**plebeians**), who themselves were bound by oath to protect the tribunes from harm. This view of tribunes as "sancrosanct," too holy to be interfered with (even by each other), was a large part of the story of the Gracchi.

What was the *Lex Sempronia Agraria*?

This was the proposal for land reform that Tiberius Gracchus made in 133 B.C. It is also called the *Lex Agraria* or Law Agraria.

Names that are easy to confuse

Gracchi or Gracchus?

Thomas North titled the whole *Life* "Tiberius and Caius Gracchi."
Dryden's translation separated the two and called them "Tiberius
Gracchus" and "Caius Gracchus." Gracchus is the singular, and
Gracchi is the plural.

Caius or Gaius?

North spelled the name Caius Gracchus, the same way that he spelled
Caius Marius and Caius Julius Caesar; and Dryden did the same.
However, Gaius is a currently acceptable English spelling.

Two Tiberiuses

Tiberius Gracchus was named for his father, who was "twice consul and
once censor," and who married Cornelia, the daughter of Scipio
Africanus (#1).

Three Scipios

Scipio Africanus the Elder (#1) was a Roman general who fought
with Hannibal in the Second Punic War; he was the father of
Cornelia and the grandfather of Tiberius and Gaius.

Scipio Africanus the Younger (#2), also called **Scipio Aemilianus**,
was **his adopted grandson**. This was the Scipio who destroyed the
city of Carthage in the Third Punic War. He married Sempronia
Gracchus, but his relationship with the Gracchi family became so
poor that, when he died suddenly, they were suspected to have
caused his death.

Publius Nasica: also called Scipio Nasica; a cousin of the Gracchi.
Nasica was Pontifex Maximus in 141 B.C. and consul in 138 B.C.

Top Vocabulary Terms

1. **commonwealth:** a state (in this case Rome) and its dependencies,
   possessions, provinces and/or colonies

2. **corn:** grain, such as wheat or barley

3. **eloquence:** the art of persuasive public speaking, especially as practiced by **orators**

4. **The Forum:** Also called **the marketplace**; the public place in Rome where speeches were made and business was done.

5. **magistrates:** elected officials

6. **meet:** proper, suitable

7. **orator:** one who makes public speeches or **orations**

8. **prefer:** propose

9. **prevail:** to succeed, win, or overcome something.

10. **pulpit, pulpit for orations:** the *Rostra*, or speaker's platform

11. **sedition:** rebellion, uprising. A **seditious** person is one who encourages rebellion.

12. **soothsayer:** one who foretells the future, often (in ancient times) by observing natural phenomena. Professional soothsayers in Rome belonged to the priesthood, and were called **augurs.**

13. **spoils:** loot, treasure. To **spoil** or **despoil** a place (such as a city or an enemy camp) is to rob it of its valuables.

14. **valiantness:** valour, meaning great courage in the face of danger, but also implying an inner force of virtue.

15. **voices:** votes

Lesson One

Introduction

Two brothers; sons of a consul and censor; grandsons of the famous Scipio Africanus (#1). Yet the biggest influence on their young lives seemed to be their mother, Cornelia, who raised and educated them with a goal of greatness.

Vocabulary

consul, censor: see introductory notes

triumph: a parade in honour of a military hero

chaste: morally upright, well behaved

choosing to die for such a woman: This does not refer to the way he died, but to a legend that he foresaw his own death, and said that it was better that he should be outlived by his (stronger) wife.

more civil, and better conditioned: "Well brought up" might be another way to put it.

Castor and Pollux: the mythological twins in the constellation Gemini

temperate: self-controlled, without extremes of behaviour

liberal: generous

mild and tractable: easygoing, even docile (able to be led)

jetted up and down the pulpit: walked back and forth on the platform

diction: manner of speaking, including vocabulary and enunciation

vehement: passionate, strong

austere: extremely plain

dolphins of silver: something for the mantelpiece, maybe?

an instrument of music: Dryden, **"a sort of pitchpipe"**

choler: anger, hot-temperedness

peradventure: perhaps

invincible: unconquerable, unbeatable

came to man's estate: became an adult

name and estimation: good reputation

People

Scipio (#1) and **(#2): see introductory notes**

King Ptolemy: Ptolemy VIII Physcon, a king of Egypt

Appius Claudius: Appius Claudius Pulcher, consul in 143 B.C.

Historic Occasions

169-163 B.C. (uncertain): Birth of Tiberius Gracchus

154 B.C.: Birth of Gaius Gracchus; death of Tiberius Sempronius Gracchus (Senior)

On the Map

As an introduction to this study, it would be good to look at a map of the Roman Republic from about the second century B.C.

Reading

Prologue

Now that we have declared unto you the history of the lives of these two Grecians, Agis and Cleomenes, we must also write the history of two Romans, the which is no less lamentable for the troubles and calamities that chanced unto Tiberius and Gaius, both of them the sons of Tiberius Sempronius Gracchus. He, having been twice **consul**, and once **censor**, and having had the honour of two **triumphs**, had notwithstanding more honour and fame only for his valiantness, for the which he was thought worthy to marry Cornelia, the daughter of **Scipio Africanus (#1)**, after Scipio's death (though there had been no friendship or familiarity between Scipio and him, but rather the contrary). *[omission]* He died, having had twelve children with Cornelia.

Cornelia after the death of her husband, taking upon her the rule of her house and children, led such a **chaste** life, was so good to her children, and of so noble a mind, that Tiberius seemed, to all men, to have done nothing unreasonable in **choosing to die for such a woman**. She remaining a widow, **King Ptolemy** made suit unto her, and would have made her his wife and queen. But she refused, and in her widowhood lost all her children, but one daughter, who was married to **the younger Scipio Africanus (#2)**, and Tiberius and Gaius, whose lives we presently write.

Part One

Those she so carefully brought up, that they became **more civil, and better conditioned**, than any other Romans in their time; every man judged that education prevailed more in them than nature. For, as in the statues and pictures of **Castor and Pollux**, there is a certain difference discerned, whereby a man may know that the one was made for wrestling, and the other for running: even so between these two young brethren, amongst other things the great likeness between them, being both happily born to be valiant, to be **temperate**, to be **liberal**, to be learned, and to be nobly minded. There grew, notwithstanding, great difference in their actions and doings in the commonwealth: the which I think convenient to declare, before I proceed any farther.

First of all, for the favour of the face, the look and moving of the body, Tiberius was much more **mild and tractable**, and Gaius more hot and earnest. For the first, in his orations, was very modest, and kept his place; and the other, of all the Romans, was the first that in his oration **jetted up and down the pulpit**, and that plucked his gown over his shoulders (as they write of Cleon the Athenian, that he was the first of all orators that opened his gown, and clapped his hand on his thigh in his oration). Gaius's oratory was impetuous and passionate, making everything tell to the utmost, whereas Tiberius was gentle and persuasive, awakening emotions of pity. His **diction** was pure and carefully correct, while that of Gaius was **vehement** and rich.

The like difference also was between them in their fare and diet. For Tiberius was frugal and plain: and Gaius also, compared with other men, temperate and even **austere**; but contrasting with his brother in a fondness for new fashions and rarities, as appeared in Drusus's charge against him that he had bought some [extremely expensive] **dolphins of silver**. The same difference that appeared in their diction was observable also in their tempers. The one was mild and reasonable, the other rough and passionate, and to that degree, that often, in the midst of speaking, he was so hurried away by his passion against his judgment, that his voice lost its tone, and he began to pass into mere abusive talking, spoiling his whole speech. Yet finding his own fault, he devised this remedy. He had a servant called Licinius, a good wise man, who had **an instrument of music**, by the which they teach men to rise and fall in their tunes. When Gaius was in his oration, Licinius ever stood behind him: and when he perceived that his master's voice was a little too loud, and that through **choler** he exceeded his ordinary speech: he played a soft note behind him, at the sound whereof Gaius immediately fell from his extremity, and easily came to himself again. Such are the differences between the two brothers; but their valour in war against their country's enemies, their justice in the government of its subjects, their care and industry in office, and their self-command in all that regarded their pleasures, were equally remarkable in both.

Tiberius was the elder by nine years; owing to which their actions as public men were divided by the difference of the times in which those of the one and those of the other were performed. And this was one of the chiefest causes why their doings prospered not, because they had not both authority in one self time, neither could they join their power together: the which if it had met at one self time, had been of great force, and **peradventure invincible**. We must therefore give an account of each of them singly, and first of the eldest.

Part Two

Tiberius, when he **came to man's estate**, had such a **name and estimation**, that immediately they made him fellow in the college of the priests, which at Rome are called augurs (those that have the charge to consider of signs and predictions of things to come), but more for his valiantness than for noble birth. The same doth **Appius Claudius** witness unto us, one that hath been both consul and censor, and also president of the Senate, and of greater authority than any man in his time. This Appius, at a supper when all the augurs were together, after he had saluted Tiberius, and made very much of him, he offered him his daughter in marriage. Tiberius was very glad of the offer, and therewithal the agreement of marriage was presently concluded between them. Thereupon Appius coming home to his house, at the threshold of his door he called aloud for his wife, and told her: "Antistia, I have contracted our daughter Claudia to a husband." She, wondering at it, "O gods," said she, "and what needed all this haste? What couldst thou have done more, if thou hadst gotten her Tiberius Gracchus for her husband?" (I am not ignorant that some apply this story to Tiberius, the father of the Gracchi, and Scipio Africanus; but most relate it as we have done *[omission]*.)

Narration and Discussion

Plutarch says that the likeness between the brothers is that they were both "happily born to be valiant, to be temperate, to be liberal, to be learned, and to be nobly minded." But he also commends their mother, because she so "carefully brought [them] up." Can both things be true?

Creative narration: Create a "wanted" or similar poster, showing the two brothers and how to tell them apart. (You may find it useful to keep this and add extra notes as you work through this *Life*.)

Lesson Two

Introduction

In this lesson we focus on the early career of Tiberius, the elder brother. He began, like many young Roman men, as a soldier in the province of Africa (serving under his brother-in-law Scipio). After winning his first position in civil government, he was sent out to deal with a crisis situation in what is now Spain: a war with the Numantines which had dragged on for years and was about to get worse.

Vocabulary

estimate: recognize and value

emulation in virtue: wanting to reach his level of courage and copy his "valiantness" (see introductory vocabulary notes)

quaestor: treasurer (an elected position, see introductory notes)

reduced to straits: in a bad situation

prevailed upon the Romans…: made sure they kept their agreement

despatched: sent

frankincense: an aromatic resin, burned as incense

base: immoral, dishonourable

impute: blame

censured: criticized, scolded

People

Fannius: Gaius Fannius Strabo, an orator and historian

Gaius Mancinus: consul in 137 B.C. After this defeat, Mancinus and other Roman commanders were ordered to be handed over to the Numantines; but (according to the historian Appian) even the Numantines refused to take him. He eventually returned to Rome, but was stripped of his seat in the Senate.

Historic Occasions

146 B.C.: Roman forces under Scipio captured and destroyed **Carthage**

143-133 B.C.: Numantine War

137 B.C.: Tiberius went to Numantia under Gaius Mancinus

134-133 B.C.: Siege of Numantia

On the Map

Carthage: a city-state in northern Africa

Numantia (Numantines): a settlement and fort north of the city of Soria, in Spain

Reading

Part One

Now Tiberius being in the wars in Africa under the younger Scipio (#2), who had married his sister, and living there under the same tent with him, soon learned to **estimate** the noble spirit of his commander, which was so fit to inspire strong feelings of **emulation in virtue**, and desire to prove merit in action. So in a short time he did excel all the young men of his time, as well in obedience as in the valiantness of his person; and he was the first to mount the walls of **Carthage**, as **Fannius** says, who writes that he himself climbed up with him, and was partaker in the achievement. He was regarded, while he continued with the army, with great affection, and left behind him on his departure a strong desire for his return.

After this war was ended, he was chosen **quaestor**, and it was his chance to go against the **Numantines**, with **Gaius Mancinus**, one of the consuls, who was an honest man, but yet had the worst luck of any captain the Romans had. Notwithstanding, Tiberius's wisdom and valiantness, in this extreme ill luck of his captain, did not only appear with great glory to him, but also most wonderful, the great obedience and reverence he bore unto his captain: though the general himself, when **reduced to straits**, forgot his own dignity and office. For being beaten in various great battles, he endeavoured to dislodge by night and leave his camp; which the Numantines perceiving, immediately possessed themselves of his camp, and pursuing that part of the forces which was in flight, slew those that were in the rear, hedged the whole army in on every side, and forced them into difficult ground, whence there could be no possibility of an escape.

Thereupon Mancinus, despairing that he could get out by force, sent a herald to the enemies to treat of peace. The Numantines made answer, that they would trust no man but Tiberius only, and therefore they willed he should be sent unto them. They desired that, partly for the love they bore unto the virtues of the young man, because there was no talk of any other in all this war but of him; and partly also, as remembering his father Tiberius, who, in his command against the Spaniards, had reduced great numbers of them to subjection, but granted a peace to the Numantines, and **prevailed upon the Romans**

to keep it punctually and inviolably.

Part Two

Tiberius was accordingly **despatched** to the enemy, whom he persuaded to accept of several conditions, and he himself complied with others; and by this means, it is beyond a question that he saved twenty thousand of the Roman citizens, besides attendants and camp followers. However, the Numantines retained possession of all the property they had found and plundered in the encampment; and amongst other things were Tiberius's books of accounts, containing all the transactions of his quaestorship. Tiberius being marvellous desirous to have his books again, returned back to Numantia with two or three of his friends only, though the army of the Romans were gone far on their way. So coming to the town, he spoke unto the governors of the city, and prayed them to redeliver him his books of account, because his malicious enemies should not accuse him, calling him to account for his doings.

The Numantines were very glad of this good hap, and prayed them to come into the town. He standing still in doubt with himself what to do, whether he should go into the town or not: the governors of the city came to him, and taking him by the hand, prayed he would think they were not his enemies, but good friends, and that he would trust them. Whereupon Tiberius thought best to yield to their persuasion, being desirous also to have his books again, and the rather, for fear of offending the Numantines, if he should have denied and mistrusted them. When he was brought into the city, they provided his dinner, and were very earnest with him, entreating him to dine with them. Then they gave him his books again, and offered him moreover to take what he would of all the spoils they had gotten in the camp of the Romans. Howbeit of all that he would take nothing but **frankincense**, which he used in his public sacrifices, and bidding them farewell with every expression of kindness, departed.

When he returned to Rome, he found the whole transaction utterly misliked, as a proceeding that was **base** and scandalous to the Romans. But the relations and friends of the soldiers, forming a large body among the people, came flocking to Tiberius, saying that what faults were committed in this service, they were to **impute** it unto the consul

Mancinus, and not unto Tiberius, who had saved such a number of Romans' lives *[omission]*.

I think Scipio (#2), who at that time was the greatest and most powerful man among the Romans, contributed to save him (Tiberius), though indeed he was also **censured** for not protecting Mancinus, too, and that he did not exert himself to maintain the observance of the articles of peace which had been agreed upon by his kinsman and friend Tiberius. But it may be presumed that the difference between them was for the most part due to ambitious feelings, and to the friends and reasoners who urged on Tiberius; and, as it was, it never amounted to anything that might not have been remedied, or that it was really bad. Nor can I think that Tiberius would ever have met with his misfortunes, if Scipio had been concerned in dealing with his measures; but he was away at the Siege of Numantia when Tiberius, upon the following occasion, first came forward as a legislator.

Narration and Discussion

When Tiberius realized that his account books were missing, what were his options? What would you have done?

Why was the peace treaty "misliked?" Does that give any hint that Tiberius might have a harder time gaining respect at home than he had with the Numantines?

Creative narration: "So in a short time he did excel all the young men of his time..." You have been asked to make a speech at Tiberius's farewell party: what will you say?

Lesson Three

Introduction

Tiberius wanted to do something about the problems he had seen inside and outside of Rome. His responsibility as tribune was to promote the rights of the common people; but his vision for reform clashed with other private interests.

Vocabulary

indigent: poor, needy

jugerum: or juger; plural jugera; a Roman unit of area. Pliny the Elder defined it as the amount of land which could be plowed by a yoke of oxen in one day. (Because there was no "j" in their alphabet, it was written *iūgerum*, and pronounced that way as well.)

bridle: stop

covetousness: wanting what one does not have

nor cared any more…: they were not so concerned about the education of their children

in all Italy: this refers to the territory outside of Rome itself

desisted: ceased, backed down

tribune of the people: see introductory note

entered upon that design: took up the same cause

who did twit her sons in the teeth: she scolded or teased them

contended with him in eloquence: rivalled him in oratorical skill

depopulated: empty of people

husbandmen: farmers

in the sequel: later on

avarice: greed

Law Agraria: *Lex Sempronia Agraria*; see introductory note

make some alteration in the state: overturn the government

confute: contradict

adversary: enemy, opponent

People

Gaius Laelius: Roman general; a friend of Scipio Africanus

Spurius Postumius: There were several similarly-named members of this family, so it's a bit uncertain which one is referred to.

Mucius Scaevola the lawyer…: Publius Mucius Scaevola was one of the consuls in 133 B.C., and he was *Pontifex Maximus* (high priest) in 131 B.C. His brother Publius Licinius **Crassus** Dives Mucianus was *Pontifex Maximus* in 132 B.C., consul in 131 B.C., and died in 130 B.C. This Crassus was also the father-in-law of Gaius Gracchus.

Historic Occasions

133 B.C.: Tiberius became tribune and proposed land reforms

On the Map

Tuscany: a region of central Italy

Reading

Part One

Of the land which the Romans gained by conquest from their neighbours, part they sold publicly, and turned the remainder into common land; this they assigned to such of the citizens as were poor and **indigent**, for which they were to pay only a small acknowledgement into the public treasury. But when the wealthy men began to offer larger rents, and drive the poorer people out, it was enacted by law that no person whatever should enjoy more than five hundred **jugera** of ground. This law for a time did **bridle** the **covetousness** of the rich men, and did ease the poor also that dwelt in the country, upon the farms they had taken up of the commonwealth, and so lived with their own, or with that their ancestors had from the beginning. Afterwards the rich of the neighbourhood contrived to get these lands again into their possession, under other people's names; and at last would not stick to claim most of them publicly in their own names.

Whereupon, the poor people being thus turned out of all, went but with faint courage afterwards to the war, **nor cared any more for bringing up of children**: so that in a short time there were comparatively few freemen remaining **in all Italy**, which swarmed with workhouses full of foreign-born slaves. These the rich men employed in cultivating their ground, of which they dispossessed the citizens.

Part Two

Gaius Laelius, one of Scipio's friends, gave an attempt to reform this abuse: but because the chiefest of the city were against him, fearing it would break out to some uproar, he **desisted** from his purpose; and therefore he was called Laelius the Wise, or the Prudent *[omission]*. But Tiberius being chosen **tribune of the people, entered upon that design** without delay, at the instigation, as is most commonly stated, of Diophanes the rhetorician and Gaius Blossius the philosopher. Diophanes was a refugee from the city of Mitylene, and Blossius an Italian from the city of Cumae (a student of Antipater of Tarsus, by whom he was honoured by certain works of philosophy he dedicated unto him).

And some also do accuse their mother Cornelia, **who did twit her sons in the teeth** that the Romans did yet call her "Scipio's mother-in-law," and not "the mother of the Gracchi."

Others say the influence on him was **Spurius Postumius**, a companion of Tiberius, and one that **contended with him in eloquence**. For Tiberius returning from the wars, and finding him far beyond him in fame and reputation, and well-beloved of everyone: he sought to excel him by attempting this noble enterprise, and of so great expectation. But his brother Gaius has left it us in writing, that when Tiberius went through **Tuscany** to Numantia, and found the country almost **depopulated**, there being hardly any free **husbandmen** or shepherds, but for the most part only barbarian, imported slaves, he then conceived the course of policy which **in the sequel** proved so fatal to his family. But in fine, it was the people only that most set his heart afire to covet honour, and that hastened his determination: first bringing him to it by bills set up on every wall, in every porch, and upon the tombs, praying him by them to cause the poor citizens of Rome to have their lands restored which were belonging to the commonwealth.

However, he did not draw up his law without the advice and assistance of those citizens that were then most eminent for their virtue and authority; amongst whom were **Crassus** the high priest, **Mucius Scaevola**, the lawyer, who at that time was consul, and Claudius Appius, his father-in-law. And truly it seemeth, that never a law was made with greater favour than that which he preferred against so great injustice and **avarice**. For those that should have been punished for transgressing the law, and should have had the lands taken from them by force, which they unjustly kept against the law of Rome, were notwithstanding to receive a price for quitting their unlawful claims, and giving up their lands to those fit owners who stood in need of help.

Part Three

Now though the reformation established by this law was done with such great favour: the people notwithstanding were contented, and were willing to forget all that was past, so that they might have no more wrong offered them in time to come. But the rich men, and men of great possessions, hated the law because of their avarice; and for spite and self-will (which would not let them yield) they were at deadly feud with the lawyer that had preferred the law, and they sought by all device they could to dissuade the people from it, telling them that Tiberius brought in this **Law Agraria** again to disturb the commonwealth, and to **make some alteration in the state**.

But they prevailed not. For Tiberius defending the matter, which of itself was good and just, with such eloquence as might have justified even an evil cause, was invincible: and no man was able to argue against him to **confute** him, when speaking in the behalf of the poor citizens of Rome. The people being gathered round about the pulpit for orations, he told them that:

> the wild beasts through Italy had their dens and
> caves of abode, and that the men that fought, and
> were slain for their country, had nothing else but air
> and light, and so were compelled to wander up and
> down with their wives and children, having no

resting place nor house to put their heads in: and that the captains do but mock their soldiers, when they encourage them in battle to fight valiantly for the graves, the temples, their own houses, and their predecessors. "For," said he, "of such a number of poor citizens as there be, there cannot a man of them show any ancient house or tomb of their ancestors: because the poor men do go to the wars, and be slain for the rich men's pleasures and wealth: besides they falsely call them lords of the earth, where they have not a handful of ground that is theirs."

These and such other like words, being uttered before all the people with such vehemence and truth, did so move the common people withal, and put them in such a rage, that there was no **adversary** of his able to withstand him.

Narration and Discussion

How did Tiberius's army travels open his eyes to the needs of those living in rural areas of Italy? What were the other influences on his movement for land reform?

For older students: and further thought The time was now ripe for more democracy in Rome, and perhaps if the Gracchi brothers had not come forward, someone else would have sparked a similar move to reform. But in a later lesson, Gaius dreams that Tiberius speaks these words to him: "One life and one death is appointed for us both, to spend the one and to meet the other in the service of the people" (Dryden's translation). Can you think of people in the Bible who were called to serve in similar ways?

Creative narration #1: Illustrate a scene from this passage.

Creative narration #2 (for older students): Write an editorial for the Rome Daily News about the unethical grabbing up of farmland.

Lesson Four

Introduction

There was a rule among the Roman tribunes that if even one of them disagreed with a proposal, the whole thing would be overthrown. Generally, this seemed to encourage teamwork and unanimity. But what could you do if a proposal was very, very important to you? And worse, what if the tribune disagreeing with you was also your friend?

Vocabulary

forbearing: skipping over; doing without

importunities: persuasions

contentions: disagreements

For not alone, etc.: Not just when you're having fun

he was not very able to perform it: it would have put a strain on his own resources

Saturn's temple: the public treasury

leave to exercise their office: refused to do their duties

changed their apparel: put on mourning clothes

deposing: removing from office

relinquish: give up

entreaty: plea

People

Marcus Octavius: an orator who was elected tribune but who was then deposed due to Tiberius's actions

Fulvius (#1): likely Gaius Fulvius Flaccus, consul in 134 B.C.

Manlius: His identity is unclear.

Historic Occasions

133 B.C.: Marcus Octavius was tribune

Reading

Part One

Forbearing, therefore, all discussion and debate, they addressed themselves to **Marcus Octavius**, his fellow-tribune, who, being a young man of a steady, orderly character, and a familiar friend of Tiberius, upon this account declined at first the task of opposing him; but at length, over-persuaded with the repeated **importunities** of numerous considerable persons, he was prevailed upon to do so, and hindered the passing of the law. For if any one of the tribunes speak against it, though all the others pass with it, he overthroweth it: because they all can do nothing, if one of them be against it.

Tiberius, irritated at these proceedings, presently laid aside this milder bill, but at the same time preferred another; which, as it was more grateful to the common people, so it was much more severe against the wrongdoers, commanding them to make an immediate surrender of all land which, contrary to former laws, had come into their possession. Hence there arose daily **contentions** between him and Octavius in their orations. However, though they were very earnest and vehement one against another, yet there passed no foul words from them, (how hot soever they were one with another) that should shame his companion.

For not alone—

   "In revellings and Bacchic play,"

but also in contentions and political animosities, a noble nature and a temperate education stay and compose the mind.

Thereupon Tiberius finding that this law, among others, touched Octavius, because he (Octavius) enjoyed a great deal of land that was the commonwealth's: he prayed him secretly to contend no more against him, promising him to give him, of his own, the value of those

174

lands which he should be driven to forsake, although **he was not very able to perform it**. But when he saw Octavius would not be persuaded, he then preferred a law that all magistrates and officers should cease their authority, till the law were either passed, or rejected, by voices of the people. He further sealed up the gates of **Saturn's temple**, so that the treasurers could neither take any money out from thence, nor put any in, upon great penalties to be forfeited by the praetors or any other magistrate of authority that should break this order. Hereupon, all the magistrates, fearing this penalty, did **leave to exercise their office** for the time. But then the rich men that were of great livings, **changed their apparel**, and walked very sadly up and down the marketplace, and laid in secret wait to take Tiberius, having hired men to kill him: which caused Tiberius himself, openly before them all, to wear a sword-staff, such as robbers use.

Part Two

When the day came that this law should be established, Tiberius called the people to give their voices: and the rich men on the other side, they took away the pots by force, wherein the papers of men's voices were thrown; thus all things were in confusion. For the party of Tiberius was the stronger side, by the number of people that were gathered about him for that purpose: had it not been for **Manlius** and **Fulvius**, both the which had been consuls *[Dryden: of consular quality]*, who went unto him, and besought him with the tears in their eyes, and holding up their hands, that he would let the law alone. Tiberius thereupon, foreseeing the instant danger of some great mischief, as also for the reverence he bore unto two such noble persons, he stayed a little, and asked them what they would have him to do. They made answer, that they were not able to counsel him in a matter of so great weight, but they prayed him notwithstanding, he would be contented to refer it to the judgement of the Senate. But afterwards perceiving that the Senate sat upon it, and had determined nothing, because the rich men were of too great authority: he entered into another course that was neither honest nor meet, which was, to deprive Octavius of his tribuneship, knowing that otherwise he could not possibly come to pass the law.

But before he took that course, he openly entreated Octavius in the face of the people with courteous words, and took him by the hand,

and prayed him to stand no more against him, and to do the people this pleasure, which required a matter just and reasonable, and only requested this final recompense for the great pains they took in service abroad for their country. Octavius denied him plainly. Then said Tiberius openly that, seeing they two were united in the same office, and of equal authority, it would be a difficult matter to compose their difference on so weighty a matter without a civil war; and that the only remedy which he knew must be **deposing** one of them from his office.

Thereupon he bade Octavius to summon the people, and begin first with him; and he would willingly **relinquish** his authority if the citizens desired it. Octavius refused; and Tiberius then said he would himself put to the people the question of Octavius's deposition, if upon mature deliberation he did not alter his mind; and after this declaration, he adjourned the assembly till the next day.

The next morning the people being again assembled, Tiberius going up to his seat, attempted again to persuade Octavius to leave off. But all being to no purpose, he referred the matter to the people, whether they were contented Octavius should be deposed from his office. Now there were five and thirty tribes of the people, of the which, seventeen of them had already passed their voices against Octavius, so that there remained but one tribe more to put him out of his office. Then Tiberius made them stay for proceeding any further, and prayed Octavius again, embracing him before all the people, with all the entreaty possible: that for self-will's sake he would not suffer such an open shame to be done unto him, as to be put out of his office: neither also to make him (Tiberius) the occasion and instrument of so pitiful a deed.

They say that Octavius at this last **entreaty** was somewhat moved and won by his persuasions; and that, weeping, he stayed a long time, and made no answer. But when he looked upon the rich men that stood in a great company together, he was ashamed (I think) to have their ill wills, and rather betook himself to the loss of his office, and so bade Tiberius do what he would. Thereupon Octavius being deprived by the voices of the people, Tiberius commanded one of his servants, whom he had made a freeman, to remove Octavius from the rostra, employing his own domestic freed servants in the stead of the public officers. This made the sight so much more lamentable, to see Octavius thus shamefully plucked away by force. Yea, furthermore, the common people would have run upon him; but the rich men came to rescue him, and would not suffer them to do him further hurt. Octavius, with some difficulty, was snatched away and safely conveyed out of the crowd *[omission]*.

Narration and Discussion

This would be a good time to review the introductory note about the sanctity of tribunes. If they were considered untouchable, not to be interfered with, why did Tiberius break that tradition?

For further thought: How can a noble *nature* and a temperate *education* help us during times of disagreement as well as during the pleasant times (the revellings)?

Creative narration: Retell the story from the point of view of Octavius.

Lesson Five

Introduction

With Octavius out of the way, Tiberius felt free to proceed with his plans; and when a large royal inheritance came into the Roman treasury, he knew just what should be done with it. However, his zeal for the poor, and his dislike for bureaucratic red tape and procedure, made some of his colleagues more uncomfortable than ever.

Vocabulary

commissioners: If you think it's odd that Tiberius was serving on his own land commission, you're not alone.

meaner: less important

obulus, pl. obuli: a silver coin

preferred a law immediately: Such a financial proposal should have been made by the senators, not by a tribune

tillage: farm land

he himself would ask their pleasure herein: he would ask the people to vote on the matter

diadem: crown

a magistrate: referring to Marcus Octavius

indicted: formally accused

sheltered himself in his own particular art: stayed with what he did best, which was asking tricky questions

defame: slander, damage one's reputation

graveled: Dryden, "disconcerted"; annoyed, irritated

arsenal: the place where weapons and ammunition are stored

when he list: when he chooses

expulsed: rejected, deposed

apology: justification for his actions

People

Publius Nasica: also called Scipio Nasica; see introductory notes

King Attalus of Pergamon: Attalus III Philometor Euergetes, the king of Pergamon, who was more interested in scholarly pursuits than in ruling. Knowing that the Romans would take his kingdom, he left it to them to avoid bloodshed. His relative Eumenes III claimed the throne and led a revolt against Rome, but it was unsuccessful.

Titus Annius: Titus Annius Luscus, consul in 153 B.C.

Historic Occasions

133 B.C.: Death of King Attalus of Pergamon

Reading

Part One

This being done, the law concerning the lands was ratified and confirmed, and three **commissioners** were appointed to make a survey of the grounds, and see the same equally divided. These were Tiberius himself; Appius Claudius, his father-in-law; and Gaius Gracchus his brother, who was not at that time in Rome, but was in the camp with Scipio Africanus (#2), at the siege of Numantia.

These things were transacted by Tiberius without any disturbance, none daring to offer any resistance to him; besides which, he gave the appointment as tribune, in Octavius's place, not to any person of distinction but to a certain Mucius, one of his own clients. Wherewith the noble men were so sore offended with him, that fearing the increase of his greatness, they took all opportunities of affronting him publicly in the Senate house. For when Tiberius demanded a tent at the charge of the commonwealth, when he should go abroad to make division of these lands, as they usually granted unto others, that many times went in far **meaner** commissions: they flatly denied him, and only granted him nine **obols** for his daily expenses. The chief promoter of these affronts was **Publius Nasica**, who openly abandoned himself to his feelings of hatred against Tiberius, being a large holder of the public lands, and not a little resenting now to be turned out of them by force. But the people, on the other hand, were all in an uproar against the rich.

[omission for length]

Part Two

About that time died **King Attalus of Pergamon**; and his official, Eudemus, brought his will to Rome, in the which he made the people of Rome his heirs. Wherefore Tiberius, still to increase the goodwill of the common people towards him, **preferred a law immediately** that the ready money that came by the inheritance of this king should be distributed among the poor citizens on whose lot it should fall to have any part of the division of the lands of the commonwealth, to furnish them towards house, and to set up their **tillage.** Furthermore, he said, that concerning the towns and cities of the kingdom of Attalus, the disposal of them did not at all belong to the Senate, but to the people, and that **he himself would ask their pleasure herein.**

That made him again more hated of the Senate than before, insomuch as there was one Pompeius, a senator, that standing up, said that he was next neighbour unto Tiberius, and so had the opportunity of knowing that Eudemus had presented Tiberius with a royal **diadem** and purple robe, as before long he was to be king of Rome. And Quintus Metellus also reproved him, saying that when Tiberius's father was censor, the Romans, whenever they happened to be going home from a supper, used to put out all their lights, lest they should be seen to have indulged themselves in feasting and drinking at unseasonable hours; whereas now, in contrary manner, the seditious and needy rabble of the common people did light his son home, and accompany him all night long up and down the town.

Titus Annius, a man of no great repute for either justice or temperance, but famous for his skill in putting and answering questions, challenged Tiberius to answer him, declaring him to have deposed **a magistrate** who by law was sacred and inviolable. Loud clamour ensued, and Tiberius, quitting the Senate hastily, called together the people, and commanded them to bring this Annius before him, that he might be **indicted** in the marketplace. But Annius, being no great speaker, nor of any repute compared to him, **sheltered himself in his own particular art**, and desired that he might propose one or two questions to Tiberius before he entered upon the chief argument. Tiberius bade him say what he would. So silence being made, Annius asked him: "If thou wouldst **defame** me, and offer me injury, and that I called one of thy colleagues to help me, and he should rise to take my part, and anger thee: wouldst thou therefore put him out of his office?"

Part Three

It is reported that Tiberius was so **graveled** with this question, that though he was one of the readiest speakers, and the boldest in his orations of any man, yet at that time he held his peace, and had no power to speak. For the present, he dismissed the assembly. But beginning to understand that the course he had taken with Octavius had created offense even among the populace as well as the nobility, because the dignity of the tribunes seemed to be violated, which had always continued till that day sacred and honourable, he made a speech to the people in justification of himself; out of which it may not be improper to collect some particulars, to give an impression of his force and persuasiveness in speaking.

> "The tribuneship," said he, "indeed was a holy and sacred thing, as particularly consecrated to the people, and established for their benefit and safety: where contrariwise, if the tribune do offer the people any wrong, he thereby diminisheth their power, and taketh away the means from them to declare their wills by voices. Besides that, he doth also imbase his own authority, leaving to do the thing for the which his authority first was given him. Or otherwise we could not choose but suffer a tribune, if it pleased him, to overthrow the Capitol, or to set fire to the **arsenal**: and yet notwithstanding this wicked part, if it were committed, he should be tribune of the people still, though a bad tribune. But when he goeth about to take away the authority and power of the people, then he is no more a tribune. Were not this against all reason, think you, that a tribune **when he list**, may take a consul, and commit him to prison: and that the people should not withstand the authority of the tribune, who gave him the same, when he would use his authority to the prejudice of the people? For the people are they that do choose both consul and tribune. Furthermore, the kingly dignity (because in the same is contained the absolute authority and power of all other kinds of magistrates and offices together) is consecrated with very great and holy ceremonies, drawing very near unto the godhead: and yet the people **expulsed** King Tarquin, because he used his authority with cruelty, and for the injury he offered one man only, the most ancient rule and

government, (by the which the foundation of Rome was first laid) was utterly abolished.

"[omission]...Nothing is so sacred as religious offerings; yet the people were never prohibited to make one of them, but suffered to remove and carry them wherever they pleased; so likewise, as it were some sacred present, they have lawful power to transfer the tribuneship from one man's hands to another's. nor can that authority be thought inviolable and irremovable which many of those who have held have of their own act surrendered and desired to be discharged from."

These were the principal heads of Tiberius's **apology**.

Narration and Discussion

Why were the senators so eager to re-open the issue of Octavius at this time?

Can you put Tiberius' speech in your own words?

For older students: It is not difficult to understand the Romans' fear of "kings," and their nervousness about those who seemed overly ambitious for power and position. They even had a word for those who leaned towards sole government control: *regnum*, or monarchism. What is harder for us to wrap our non-Roman minds around is their suspicion of anyone who seemed to be too interested in the problems of the poor. Can you follow their thinking on this? How did that put Tiberius in a difficult position?

Lesson Six

Introduction

Tiberius was informed that there were finally enough supporters assembled to pass the laws he had proposed, and he headed for the

Capitol. Because of extreme miscommunication during the assembly, a group of senators, protesting the refusal of the consul to have Tiberius arrested, incited a riot.

Vocabulary

Roman knights: those of the Equestrian social class, ranking below the Patricians. In time of war, these were the men who would make up the cavalry, because they were wealthy enough to own horses.

partisanship: favouritism

prognosticate: foretell, predict

felt as check: thought to be a warning

truncheons: clubs

intimate: communicate

coat: tunic, undergarment

People

Blossius, the philosopher of Cumae: mentioned in **Lesson Three**

Flavius Flaccus: Marcus Fulvius Flaccus, known for his support of the Gracchi

Historic Occasions

133 B.C.: Death of Tiberius

Reading

Part One

Now Tiberius's friends perceiving the threats the rich and noble men gave out against him, they wished him, for the safety of his person, to make suit to be tribune again the next year. Upon this consideration he again endeavoured to secure the people's goodwill with fresh laws, making the years of serving in the war fewer than formerly, granting liberty of appeal from the judges to the people, and joining to the senators, who were judges at that time, a like number of the **Roman knights**, endeavouring as much as in him to lessen the power of the Senate, increasing also the power of the people, rather from passion and **partisanship** than from any rational regard to equity and the public good. And when it came to the question whether these laws should be passed, and they perceived that the opposite party were strongest, the people as yet being not got together in a full body, they began first of all to gain time by speeches in accusation of some of their fellow magistrates; and at length adjourned the assembly till the day following.

Tiberius then went down into the marketplace amongst the people, appareled all in black, his face beblubbered with tears, and looking heavily upon the matter, praying the people assembled to have compassion upon him, saying that he was afraid lest his enemies would come in the night, and overthrow his house to kill him. Thereupon the people were so moved withal, that many of them came and brought their tents, and lay about his house to watch it. By break of day came one of the soothsayers, who **prognosticate** good or bad success by the pecking of fowls, and threw them something to eat. None of the birds would come out of the cage but one only, and yet with much ado, shaking the cage: and when it came out, it would eat nothing, but only lift up her left wing, and put forth her leg, and so ran into the cage again. This sign made Tiberius remember another he had had before. He had a marvellous fair helmet and very rich, which he wore in the wars: under it were crept two snakes unawares to any, and they laid eggs, and brought forth young ones. This made Tiberius wonder the more, because of the ill signs of the chickens.

Notwithstanding, he went out of his house, when he heard that the people were assembled in the Capitol; but as he went out, he hit his foot such a blow against a stone at the threshold of the door, that he broke the nail of his great toe, which fell in such a-bleeding, that it bled through his shoe. Again, he had not gone far, but he saw upon the top of a house on his left hand, a couple of ravens fighting together; and notwithstanding that there passed a great number of people by, yet a stone which one of these ravens cast from them, came and fell hard at

Tiberius's foot. This even the boldest men about him **felt as check**. But **Blossius, the philosopher of Cumae** that did accompany him, told him it were a great shame for him, and enough to kill the hearts of all his followers, that Tiberius being the son of Gracchus, and grandson of Scipio Africanus (#1), and the chief man besides of all the people's side, for fear of a raven, should not obey his citizens that called him; and how that his enemies and ill-willers would not make a laughing sport of it, but would plainly tell the people that this was a trick of a tyrant that reigned indeed, and that for pride and disdain did abuse the people's goodwill.

Part Two

At the same time several messengers came also from his friends, to desire his presence at the Capitol, saying that all things went there according to expectation. When he came thither, he was honourably received: for the people seeing him coming, cried out for joy to welcome him, and when he was gotten up to his feet, they showed themselves both careful and loving towards him, looking warily that none came near him, but such as they knew well. While Mucius began again to call the tribes of the people to give their voices, he could not proceed according to the accustomed order, for the great noise the hindmost people made, thrusting forward, and being driven back, and one mingling with another.

While things were in this confusion, **Flavius Flaccus**, a senator, standing in a place where he could be seen, but at such a distance from Tiberius that he could not make him hear, made a sign with his hand that he had some matter of great importance to tell him. Tiberius ordered the multitude to make way for him, by which means, though not without some difficulty, Flavius got to him, and informed him that the rich men, in a sitting of the Senate, seeing they could not prevail upon the consul to espouse their quarrel, had come to a final determination amongst themselves that he should be assassinated, and to that purpose had a great number of their friends and servants ready armed to accomplish it. Tiberius no sooner communicated this conspiracy to those about him, but they immediately tucked up their gowns, broke the **truncheons** (which the officers used to keep the crowd off) into pieces, and distributed those among themselves, resolving to resist the attack with these. Those who stood at a distance wondered, and asked what was the occasion; Tiberius, knowing that they could not hear him at that distance, lifted his hand to his head, wishing to **intimate** the great danger which he apprehended himself to be in.

His enemies seeing the sign he gave, ran presently to the Senate, and declared that Tiberius desired the people to bestow a crown upon him, as if this were the meaning of his touching his head. This news created general confusion in the senators, and Nasica at once called upon the consul to punish this tyrant, and defend the government. The consul mildly replied that he would use no force, neither put any citizen to death, but lawfully condemned: as also he would not receive Tiberius, nor protect him, if the people by his persuasion or commandment, should commit any act contrary to the law.

Nasica then rising in anger, "Since the matter is so," said he, "that the consul regardeth not the commonwealth: all you then, that will defend the authority of the law, follow me." Thereupon he cast the skirt of his gown over his head, and went straight to the Capitol; those who bore him company, wrapped their gowns also about their arms, and forced their way after him.

As they were persons of the greatest authority in the city, the common people did not venture to obstruct their passing, but were rather so eager to clear the way from them, that they tumbled over one another in haste. The attendants they brought with them had furnished themselves with clubs and staves from their houses, and they themselves picked up the feet and other fragments of stools and chairs, which were broken by the hasty flight of the common people. Thus armed, they made towards Tiberius, knocking down those whom they found in front of him, and those were soon wholly dispersed, and many of them slain.

Tiberius seeing that, betook him to his legs to save himself, but as he was fleeing, one took him by the gown, and stayed him: but he, leaving his gown behind him, ran in his **coat**, and running, fell upon them that were down before. So as he was rising up again, the first man that struck him, and that was plainly seen to strike him, was one of the tribunes his brethren, called Publius Satureius, who gave him a great rap on the head with the foot of a chair; and the second blow he had was given him by Lucius Rufus, that boasted of it as if he had done a notable act. In this tumult, there were slain above three hundred men, and they were all killed with clubs and staves, and not one man was hurt with any iron weapon.

Narration and Discussion

In Part One, what were some of the new laws that Tiberius proposed? What was the purpose of his dramatics in the forum? Did Tiberius really believe that he was in danger?

How does Part Two parallel the *Life of Julius Caesar*? Can you predict how the people of Rome would react to the death of Tiberius?

Creative narration: You are a reporter for the Rome Daily News. If you are working with a group, you may interview onlookers at the scene of the riot; or simply write the news story.

Lesson Seven

Introduction

After the riot and the death of Tiberius Gracchus, Rome was in shock. According to Plutarch, it was "the first sedition among the citizens of Rome that fell out with murder and bloodshed, since the expulsion of the kings." Who was at fault? Was it safer to support Tiberius, or to say that he had brought his fate on himself?

Vocabulary

since the expulsion of the kings: in the entire history of the Roman Republic

amicably composed: settled without anger

mutual concessions: when both sides agree to give up certain demands

made earnest suit: pleaded

law Agraria: law regarding the distribution of land (see introductory notes)

impeachment: removal from office for misconduct

ignominiously: in shame

meanly: plainly, simply

in the commonwealth: in public affairs

antipathy: hatred, aversion

he had such an eloquent tongue: he was so well-spoken

all the orators besides: the other speakers

martial: military

prayed his furtherance: wanted his help

private man: one not holding any public office

predestined: fated or designed before birth

People

Aristonicus: the original name of **Eumenes III** of Pergamon

Publius Crassus: see **Lesson Three**

Orestes, the consul: Lucius Aurelius Orestes, consul in 126 B.C. and then proconsul in Sardinia

Historic Occasions

132 B.C.: Death of Nasica

126 B.C.: Gaius Gracchus was chosen quaestor

On the Map

Sardinia: a large island west of the Italian peninsula, south of Corsica

Reading

Part One

This was the first sedition among the citizens of Rome that fell out with murder and bloodshed, **since the expulsion of the kings**. All former quarrels, which were neither small nor about trivial matters, were always **amicably composed**, by **mutual concessions** on either side, the Senate yielding for fear of the commons, and the commons out of respect to the Senate. And it seemeth that Tiberius himself might have been easily induced, by mere persuasion, to give way; and certainly, if attacked at all, must have yielded without any recourse to violence and bloodshed, as he had not at that time above three thousand men to support him. But surely it seems this conspiracy was executed against him more for very spite and malice the rich men did bear him, than for any other apparent cause they presupposed against him.

For proof hereof may be alleged, the barbarous cruelty they used to his body, being dead. For they would not suffer his own brother to have his body to bury it by night, who **made earnest suit** unto them for it: but they threw him amongst the other bodies into the river.

Blossius also, the philosopher of Cumae, was brought before the consuls, and examined about this matter: who boldly confessed unto them, that he did as much as Tiberius commanded him. When Nasica did ask him, "And what if he had commanded thee to set fire on the Capitol?" he gave answer that Tiberius would never have given him any such commandment. And when divers others also were still in hand with him about that question: "But if he had commanded thee?" "I would sure have done it," said he. "For he would never have commanded me to have done it, if it had not been for the people's good." Thus he escaped at that time, and afterwards fled into Asia unto **Aristonicus**, and when Aristonicus was overthrown and ruined, killed himself.

Now the Senate, to pacify the people at that present time, did no more withstand the **law Agraria**, for division of the lands of the commonwealth, but suffered the people to appoint another commissioner for that purpose, in Tiberius's place. So they elected **Publius Crassus**, who was a near connection of the Gracchi, as his daughter Licinia was married to Gaius Gracchus (although Cornelius Nepos says that it was not Crassus's daughter whom Gaius married, but Brutus's, who triumphed for his victories over the Lusitanians; but most writers state it as we have done).

But whatsoever was done, the people were marvellously offended with his death, and men might easily perceive that they looked but for time and opportunity to be revenged, and Nasica was already threatened with an **impeachment**. The Senate, therefore, fearing lest some mischief should befall him, sent him ambassador into Asia, though there was no occasion for his going thither. For the people did not conceal their indignation, even in the open streets, but railed at him whenever they met him abroad, calling him a murderer and a tyrant, one who had polluted the most holy and religious spot in Rome with the blood of a sacred and inviolable magistrate. And so Nasica left Italy, although he was bound, being the chief priest, to officiate in all principal sacrifices. Thus wandering wretchedly and **ignominiously** from one place to another, he died in a short time after.

[Omission for length]

Part Two

Now Gaius Gracchus at the first, because he feared the enemies of his dead brother, or otherwise for that he sought means to make them more hated of the people: he absented himself for a time out of the common assembly, and kept at home and meddled not, as a man contented to live **meanly**, without busying himself **in the commonwealth**; insomuch as he made men think and report both, that he did utterly mislike those matters which his brother had preferred. Howbeit he was then but a young man, and nine years younger than his brother Tiberius, who was not thirty years old when he was slain.

In some little time, however, he quietly let his temper appear, which was one of an utter **antipathy** to a lazy retirement and [attention to personal comfort], and not the least likely to be contented with a life of eating, drinking, and money-getting. He gave great pains to the study of eloquence, as wings upon which he might aspire to public business; and it was very apparent that he did not intend to pass his days in obscurity. When Vettius, a friend of his, was on his trial, he defended his cause. The people that were present, and heard him speak, they leaped for joy to see him: for **he had such an eloquent tongue**, that **all the orators besides** were but children to him. Hereupon the rich men began to be afraid again, and whispered among themselves, that they must hinder Gaius from being made tribune.

But soon after, it happened that he was elected quaestor, and obliged to attend **Orestes, the consul**, into **Sardinia**. His enemies were glad of that, and he himself was not sorry for it. For he was a **martial** man, and as skillful in arms as he was else an excellent orator: but yet he was afraid to come into the pulpit for orations, and misliked to deal in matters of state, albeit he could not altogether deny the people, and his friends that **prayed his furtherance**. For this cause therefore he was very glad of this voyage, that he might absent himself for a time out of Rome: though some were of opinion that he was more popular, and desirous of the common people's good will and favour, than his brother had been before him. Yet it is certain that he was borne rather by a sort of necessity than by any purpose of his own into public business.

Cicero the orator also sayeth that Gaius was bent altogether to flee from office in the commonwealth, and to live quietly as a **private man**. But Tiberius (Gaius's brother) appeared to him in his sleep, and calling him by his name, said unto him: "Brother, why dost thou prolong time, for thou canst not possibly escape? For we were both **predestined** to one manner of life and death, for procuring the benefit of the people."

Narration and Discussion

Why did Gaius live so quietly for a while, even against his own natural gifts and interests? How did he need to prepare before taking up his brother's causes? You may wish to go back to the profile of Gaius that you wrote in Lesson One.

What qualities did Gaius display that made rich men afraid of him, but made other people desire his leadership?

For further thought: How might eloquence give one wings?

Creative narration: As a reporter for the Rome Daily News, you have been given an exclusive interview with Gaius Gracchus. What questions will you ask him? Write or act out the conversation.

Lesson Eight

Introduction

Like his brother before him, Gaius Gracchus sometimes did the right things in wrong ways, or at least in ways that created jealousy or suspicion. The problem this time was with supplies for the army. Who had sent them, in Gaius's opinion, was not as important as keeping the soldiers fed; what did it matter if they came from a foreign king who "owed him one?" But Gaius showed himself surprisingly able to handle this kind of trouble; maybe things would go better this time around.

Vocabulary

exemplary: outstanding

industry: hard work

their allegation: their excuse for not complying

smarted: suffered

censure: criticism

insurrection: rebellion

Field of Mars: the *Campus Martius*, a large area which at this time was open space used for political or military events. Later, parts of the land were sold to private owners, and buildings were erected on it such as the Pantheon.

let: prevent

scurrilous: rude

should pertain to the people: the citizens should have a say in it

diminution: decrease

Comitium: an open-air meeting space in the Roman Forum

People

King Micipsa: the king of Numidia (a kingdom of northwest Africa)

Popilius: Publius Popillius Laenas, consul in 132 B.C

Historic Occasions

123-122 B.C.: Gaius Gracchus was tribune in both years

Reading

Part One

Gaius was no sooner arrived in Sardinia, but he gave **exemplary** proofs of his high merit; he not only excelled all the young men of his age in his actions against his enemies, in doing justice to his inferiors, and in showing all obedience and respect to his superior officer; but likewise in temperance, frugality, and **industry**, he surpassed those who were much older than himself.

The winter by chance fell out very sharp, and full of sickness in Sardinia: whereupon the consul sent into the cities to help his soldiers with some clothes; but the towns sent in post to Rome, to pray the Senate they might be discharged of that burden. The Senate found **their allegation** reasonable, whereupon they wrote to the consul to find some other means to clothe his people. The consul could make no other shift for them, and so the poor soldiers in the meantime **smarted** for it. But Gaius Gracchus went himself unto the cities and so persuaded them, that they of themselves sent to the Romans' camp such things as they lacked. This being carried to Rome, it was thought straight it was a pretty beginning to creep into the peoples' favour, and indeed it raised new jealousies among the senators. In the neck of that, there arrived ambassadors of Africa at Rome, sent from **King**

Micipsa, who told the Senate that the king their master, for Gaius Gracchus's sake, had sent their army corn into Sardinia.

The senators were so offended withal, that they thrust the ambassadors out of the Senate, and so gave order that other soldiers should be sent in the place of those that were in Sardinia; but that Orestes should continue at his post, with whom Gaius, also, as they presumed, being his quaestor, would remain. But he, finding how things were carried, immediately in anger took ship for Rome, where his unexpected appearance obtained him the **censure** not only of his enemies, but also of the people; who thought it strange that a quaestor should leave before his commander.

He being accused hereof before the censors, prayed he might be heard. So, answering his accusation, he so turned the people's minds that heard him, that they all said he had been very much injured. For he told them that he had served twelve years in the wars, where others were enforced to remain but ten years; and that he had continued treasurer under his captain for the space of three years, where the law gave him liberty to return at the end of the year. And that he alone of all men else that had been in the wars, had carried his purse full, and brought it home empty; where others having drunk the wine which they carried thither in vessels, had afterwards brought them home full of gold and silver.

Part Two

After this they brought other accusations and writs against him; for exciting **insurrection** amongst the allies, and being engaged in a conspiracy that was revealed in the city of Fregellae. But having cleared all that suspicion, and being discharged, he presently made suit to be tribune: wherein he had all the men of quality as his sworn enemies. On the other side also he had so great favour of the common people, that there came men out of all parts of Italy to be at his election, and that such a number of them, as there was no lodging to be had for them all. Furthermore, the **Field of Mars** not being large enough to hold such a multitude of people, there were that gave their voices upon the top of houses.

Now the noblemen could no otherwise **let** the people of their will, nor prevent Gaius of his hope, but where he thought to be the first tribune, he was only pronounced the fourth.

But when he came to the execution of his office, it was seen presently who was really first tribune, as he was a better orator than any of his contemporaries, and the passion with which he still lamented his brother's death made him the bolder in speaking. He used on all occasions to remind the people of what had happened in that tumult, and laid before them the example of their ancestors, how they declared war against the Faliscans only for giving **scurrilous** language to one Genucius, a tribune of the people; and sentenced Gaius Veturius to death, for refusing to give way in the Forum to a tribune.

> "Whereas these," said he, "that standing before you in sight, have slain my brother Tiberius with staves, and have dragged his body from the Mount of the Capitol, all the city over, to throw it into the river: and with him also have most cruelly slain all his friends they could come by, without any law or justice at all. And yet by an ancient custom of long time observed in this city of Rome, when any man is accused of treason, and that of duty he must appear at the time appointed him: they do notwithstanding in the morning send a trumpet to his house, to summon him to appear: and moreover the Judges were not wont to condemn him, before this ceremony was performed: so careful and respectful were our predecessors, where it touched the life of any Roman."

Part Three

Now Gaius having first stirred up the people with these persuasions (for he had a marvellous loud voice) he preferred two laws. The first, that whoever had once been put out of office by the people, should never after be capable of any other office. The second, that if any consul had banished any citizen without a legal trial, the sentence and hearing of the matter **should pertain to the people**. The first of these two laws did plainly defame Octavius, whom Tiberius his brother had by the people deposed from the tribuneship. The second also touched **Popilius**, who, in his praetorship, had banished all his brother

Tiberius's friends. Whereupon Popilius, being unwilling to stand the hazard of a trial, fled out of Italy. And touching the first law, Gaius himself did afterwards revoke it, declaring unto the people that he yielded in the case of Octavius, at the request of his mother Cornelia. The people were very glad of it, and confirmed it, honouring her no less for respect of her sons, than also for Scipio's sake, her father. For afterwards they cast her image in brass, and set it up with this inscription: "Cornelia, the mother of the Gracchi." Many common matters are found written, touching Cornelia his mother, and eloquently pleaded in her behalf by Gaius against her adversaries. As when he said unto one of them: "How darest thou presume to speak evil of Cornelia, that had Tiberius to her son?" Thus were Gaius's words sharp and stinging, and many such like are to be gathered out of his writings.

Of the laws which he now proposed, with the object of gratifying the people and weakening the power of the Senate, the first was concerning the public lands, which were to be divided amongst the poor citizens; another was concerning the common soldiers, that they should be clothed at the public charge, without any **diminution** of their pay; and that none should be obliged to serve in the army who was not full seventeen years old. Another law was for their confederates of Italy: that through all Italy they should have as free voices in the election of any magistrate, as the natural citizens of Rome itself.

A fourth related to the price of corn, which was to be sold at a lower rate than formerly to the poor; and a fifth regulated the courts of justice, greatly reducing the power of the senators. For before, the senators were the only judges of all matters, and were therefore much dreaded by the Roman knights and the people. But Gaius joined three hundred ordinary citizens of equestrian rank with the senators, who were three hundred likewise in number, so that all matters judicial should be equally judged among those six hundred men.

After he had passed this law, it is reported he showed unusual earnestness in observing all other things, but this one thing specially: that where all other orators speaking to the people turned themselves towards the palace where the senators sat, and to that side of the marketplace which is called *Comitium*: he in contrary manner when he made his oration, turned him outwards towards the other side of the marketplace, and after that kept it constantly, and never failed. Thus, by a little turning and altering of his look only, he removed a great matter. For he so transferred all the government of the commonwealth from the Senate, unto the judgement of the people: to teach the orators by his example, that in their orations they should behold the people, not the Senate.

Narration and Discussion

Compare the description of Gaius in the first paragraph with what we have been previously told of him. Does it sound like he has changed?

How did Gaius successfully defend himself on his return from Sardinia?

For further thought: Gaius changed the direction in which he gave his speeches. Why did this signal a change of direction for the government?

Creative narration: You are the editor of the Rome Women's Magazine (you can give it a better name), and you have decided to do a cover story about Cornelia. You can do just one part of the project that appeals to you, such as the cover art or an interview; or a group might assign artists and writers to complete the whole project.

Lesson Nine

Introduction

"Now, the people having not only confirmed the law he made regarding the judges, but given him also full power and authority to choose among the Roman knights such judges as he liked of: he found thereby he had absolute power in his own hands, insomuch as the senators themselves did ask counsel of him." Gaius used his power to build mend roads, re-people colonies, and refuse tribute from Spain that would impoverish the people there. But admiration was turning to jealousy, and a conspiracy arose against him.

Vocabulary

derogate from: detract from, take away

a good and honourable act: not the sending of the wheat, but Gaius's refusal of it

commendation: praise

granaries: barns to hold grain

those were looked upon as no better…: Because Gaius showed himself to be such a good leader, it was assumed that anyone who had said bad things about him must have been merely jealous and spiteful.

extolled: praised

canvassing: asking for support for a cause

slack: unfaithful

the same privileges: the privileges of Roman citizenship such as voting, and receiving subsidized grain

playing the demagogue: trying to get votes or support by appealing to people's emotions and prejudices

with such unreasonable things…: An analogy, though we hope this should never happen: a child has asked for an unsuitable toy as a birthday gift, which gives both of its parents an opportunity to prove what a good parents they are by saying "no," and so it appears the issue is closed. One of the parents wraps up several nice educational toys for the birthday. However, the other parent persuades Grandma to buy the requested toy, thereby making the first parent now seem both a tyrant for insisting that it be sent back.

obsequious: using insincere flattery; "boot-licking"

People

Fabius the vice praetor: Quintus Fabius Maximus Allobrogicus, the governor of Spain in 123 B.C., and consul two years later

Gaius Fannius: Gaius Fannius Strabo, elected consul for 122 B.C.

Livius Drusus: Marcus Livius Drusus, appointed tribune for the sole purpose of counter-offering anything that Gaius Gracchus proposed

On the Map

Tarentum (Tarentines): or Tarento; a city in Apulia, Italy

Capua: a city in the region of Campania, in southern Italy

Reading

Part One

Now, the people having not only confirmed the law Tiberius made regarding the judges, but having given him also full power and authority to choose among the Roman knights such judges as he liked: he found thereby he had absolute power in his own hands, insomuch as the senators themselves did ask counsel of him; nor did he advise anything that might **derogate from** the honour of that body. As, amongst others, the law he made touching certain corn that **Fabius the vice praetor** had sent out of Spain: which was **a good and honourable act**. He persuaded the Senate that the corn might be sold, and so to send back again the money thereof unto the towns and cities from whence the corn came: and that they should punish Fabius because he made the empire of Rome hateful and intolerable unto the provinces and subjects of the same. This matter won him great love and **commendation** of all the provinces subject to Rome. Furthermore, he made laws for the restoring of the decayed towns, for mending of highways, for building of public **granaries**; of all which works he himself undertook the management and superintendence, and was never wanting to give necessary orders for the dispatch of all these different and great undertakings. For he followed all those things so earnestly and effectually, as if he had had but one master in hand: insomuch that they who most hated and feared him wondered most to see his diligence and quick dispatch in matters.

The people also wondered much to behold him only, seeing always such a number of labourers, artificers, ambassadors, officers, soldiers, and learned men. All these he treated with an easy familiarity, yet without abandoning his dignity in his gentleness; and so accommodated his nature to the wants and occasions of everyone who addressed him, that **those were looked upon as no better than envious detractors who had represented him as a terrible, assuming, and violent character**. Thus he won the good will of the common people, being more popular and familiar in his conversation and deeds than he was otherwise in his orations.

But the greatest pains and care he took upon him was in seeing the highways mended, which he was careful to make beautiful and pleasant, as well as convenient. They were drawn by his directions through the fields, exactly in a straight line, partly paved with hewn stone, and partly laid with solid masses of gravel. When he met with any valleys or deep watercourses crossing the line, he either caused them to be filled up with rubbish, or bridges to be built over them, so well levelled, that all being of an equal height on both sides, the work presented one uniform and beautiful prospect. Furthermore, he divided these highways by miles, every mile containing eight furlongs, and at every mile's end, he set up a stone for a mark. At either end also of these highways thus paved, he set certain stones of convenient height at small distances from one another, to help the travellers-by to take their horses' backs again, without any help.

For these reasons, the people highly **extolled** him, and were ready upon all occasions to express their affection towards him. One day, in an oration to them, he declared that he had only one favour to request, which, if they granted, he should think the greatest obligation in the world; yet if it were denied, he would never blame them for the refusal. Then every man thought it was the consulship he meant to ask, and that he would sue to be tribune and consul together. But when the day came to choose the consuls, every man looking attentively what he would do: they marvelled when they saw him come down the Field of Mars with Gaius Fannius, **canvassing** together with his friends for his (Fannius's) election. This was of great effect in Fannius's favour. He was chosen consul, and Gaius was elected tribune the second time, without his own seeking or petitioning for it, but by the goodwill of the people.

Part Two

But when he understood that the senators were his open enemies, and that Fannius the consul was but a **slack** friend unto him, he began again to curry favour with the common people, and to prefer new laws, setting forth the law of the colonies, that they should send some of the poor citizens to replenish the cities of **Tarentum** and **Capua**; and that they should grant all the Latins **the same privileges** with the citizens of Rome.

The Senate perceiving his power grew great, and that in the end he would be so strong that they could not withstand him: they devised a new and strange way to pluck the people's goodwill from him, by **playing the demagogue** in opposition to him, and offering favours contrary to all good policy. There was one of the tribunes, a brother in office with Gaius, called **Livius Drusus**, a man nobly born, and as well brought up as any other Roman: who for wealth and eloquence was not inferior to the greatest men of estimation in Rome. The chiefest senators went unto him, and persuaded him to take part with them against Gaius, not to use any force or violence against the people to withstand them in anything, but contrarily by gratifying and obliging them (the common people) **with such unreasonable things as otherwise the senators would have felt it honourable for them to incur the greatest unpopularity in resisting**.

Livius offered to serve the Senate with his authority in this business; and proceeded accordingly to bring forward such laws as were in reality neither honourable nor advantageous for the public; his whole design being to outdo Gaius in pleasing and cajoling the populace (as if it had been in some comedy) with **obsequious** flattery and every kind of gratifications; the Senate thus letting it be seen plainly that they were not angry with Gaius's public measures, but only desirous to ruin him utterly, or at least to lessen his reputation.

For where Gaius preferred but the replenishing of the two cities, and desired to send the honestest citizens thither: they objected against him, that he did corrupt the common people. On the other side, also they favoured Livius Drusus, who preferred a law that they should replenish twelve colonies, and should send to every one of them three thousand of the poorest citizens. And where they hated Gaius for that he had charged the poor citizens with an annual rent for the lands that were divided unto them: Livius in contrary manner did please them by disburdening them of that rent and payment, letting them have the lands scot free. The people were displeased with Gaius for offering the Latins an equal right with the Romans of voting at the election of magistrates; but when Livius proposed that it might not be lawful for a Roman captain to scourge a Latin soldier, they promoted the passing of that law.

[Omission for length: Livius's campaign to promote the "friendly Senate" to the common people was quite successful.]

Narration and Discussion

In Part One, Gaius supported his friend Gaius Fannius in the election for consul. By Part Two, Fannius is called a "slack friend." What might have happened during that time?

Explain the game of one-upmanship that the senators began against Gaius. Did they actually dislike the things he was proposing?

For older students: North's choice of phrase "as if he had had but one master in hand" has interesting connotations; but Dryden translates it "as if he had been but engaged upon one undertaking." Both translations echo what Charlotte Mason described in her book *Ourselves*: "The simple, rectified Will, what our Lord calls 'the single eye,' would appear to be the one thing needful for straight living and serviceableness." What are the benefits, and possibly the dangers, of such single-mindedness?

Lesson Ten

Introduction

Marcus Fulvius Flaccus was involved in the administration of the *Lex Agraria*; had been a consul for a year and earned a military triumph; and finally took the unusual step of becoming a tribune so that he could support the proposals of Gaius Gracchus. But his loyalty to

Gaius became a threat to his own safety, and vice versa.

Vocabulary

staff of his ensign: a banner carried on a pole

ordered and despatched: completed

the present juncture of affairs: the current situation

set Gaius beside the saddle: get him out of the way

Mount Palatine: a wealthy district of Rome

allies or confederates: those from other parts of the commonwealth

People

Fulvius: see **Lesson Six**

Lucius Opimius: consul in 121 B.C.

Fannius: see **Lesson Nine**

Historic Occasions

129 B.C.: Death of Scipio Africanus (#2)

125 B.C.: Marcus Fulvius Flaccus was consul

122 B.C.: Fulvius became tribune

Reading

Part One

Rubrius, another tribune of the people, had proposed to have Carthage again inhabited, which had been demolished; it fell to Gaius's lot to see this performed, and for that purpose he sailed to Africa. Livius Drusus in the meantime, taking occasion of his absence, did as much as might be to seek the favour of the common people, and specially by accusing **Fulvius**, who was one of the best friends Gaius had, and whom they had also chosen commissioner with him for the division of the lands. This Fulvius was a man of a turbulent spirit, and notoriously hated by the Senate; and besides, he was suspected by others to have fomented the difference between the citizens and their confederates, and underhand to be inciting the Italians to rebel; though there was little other evidence of the truth of these accusations than his being an unsettled character and of a well-known seditious temper. This was one principal cause of Gaius's ruin; for part of the envy which fell upon Fulvius was extended to him.

A flashback

For when Scipio Africanus (#2) was found dead one morning in his house, without any manifest cause how he should come to his death so suddenly (only some marks of blows upon his body seemed to intimate that he had suffered violence, as we have declared in his *Life*) the most part of the suspicion of his death was laid to Fulvius, being his mortal enemy, and because the same day they had been at great words together in the pulpit for orations. So was Gaius Gracchus also partly suspected for it. Howsoever it was, such a horrible murder as this, of so famous and worthy a man as any was in Rome, was yet notwithstanding never revenged, neither any inquiry made of it: because the common people would not suffer the accusation to go forward, fearing lest Gaius would be found in fault, if the matter should go forward. But this was a great while before.

Part Two

But in Africa, where at present Gaius was engaged in the re-peopling of Carthage, which he named "Junonia," many ominous appearances, which foretold mischief, are reported to have been sent from the gods. For the **staff of his ensign** was broken with a vehement blast of wind, and with the force of the ensign bearer that held it fast on the other side. There came a sudden storm also that carried away the sacrifices upon the altars, and blew them quite out of the circuit which was marked out for the compass of the city. Furthermore, the wolves came and carried away the very marks that were set up to show the boundary.

Gaius, notwithstanding all this, **ordered and despatched** the whole business in the space of seventy days, and then returned to Rome, understanding how Fulvius was prosecuted by Livius Drusus, and that **the present juncture of affairs** would not suffer him to be absent. For **Lucius Opimius**, one who sided with the nobility, and was of no small authority in the Senate, who had formerly sued to be consul, but was repulsed by Gaius's interest at the time when **Fannius** was elected, was in a fair way now of being chosen consul, having a numerous company of supporters. So that if he could obtain it, he was fully bent to **set Gaius beside the saddle**, whose power was already in a declining condition; and the people were not so apt to admire his actions as formerly, because there were so many others who every day contrived new ways to please them, with which the Senate readily complied.

So Gaius being returned to Rome, where before he dwelt in **Mount Palatine**, he came now to take a house near the marketplace, to show himself thereby the lowlier and more popular, because many of the meaner sort of people dwelt thereabouts. He then brought forward the remainder of his proposed laws, as intending to have them ratified by the popular vote; and to support this, a vast number of people collected from all quarters. But the Senate persuaded Fannius, the consul, to command all persons who were not born Romans to depart the city. A new and unusual proclamation was made, prohibiting any of the **allies or confederates** from appearing at Rome during that time. Gaius, on the contrary, published an edict accusing Fannius for what he had done, and setting forth to the confederates that if they would continue upon the place, they might be assured of his assistance and protection.

However, he was not so good as his word, for though he saw one of his own familiar friends and companions dragged to prison by Fannius's officers, he, notwithstanding, passed by without assisting him; either because he was afraid to stand the test of his power, which was already decreased, or because, as he himself reported, he was unwilling (as he said) to pick any quarrel with his enemies, which sought it of him.

Narration and Discussion

How did Gaius's friendship with Fulvius affect his own standing in Rome? What other reasons are given for the decline in his popularity?

Creative narration #1: As the editor of the Rome Women's Magazine, you have decided to do a feature story about Licinia, the wife of Gaius Gracchus, and their new home. As before, you might choose to do only the cover, or show some "photos."

Creative narration #2: Draw a political cartoon that might have appeared in the Rome Daily News at this time.

Lesson Eleven

Introduction

Now that Gaius was no longer tribune, the Senate felt free to revoke his laws, apparently hoping to provoke him into violent or illegal action. Gaius held out patiently for as long as he could, but the tension in Rome was mounting. When a rude remark blew into a fight and then murder, the frightened Senate put the city under full control of the new consul, Opimius.

Vocabulary

scaffolds: grandstands; raised seating (which also obscured the view of the bystanders)

presumptuous: going too far beyond accepted behaviour

he was put from his third tribuneship: he was not re-elected

returns: election results; counts of the votes

sardonic: mocking, cynical, ironic. Gaius seemed to be saying, "Soon you'll be laughing on the other side of your face," meaning that things would move in his favour again.

intimations: hints

revocation: formal cancellation

bodkins to write with: Death by writing implement sounds strange, but Roman styluses could be sharp.

bier: a frame on which a corpse is carried (like a stretcher)

the occasion of it himself: he had brought it on himself

invested with extraordinary power: *Senatus consultum ultimum*, or "Final Act"; a lifting of limits on magisterial power that had never been used before

upbraid: scold

Gauls: tribes of northern Europe

at such a strait: at such a dangerous time

made their way towards Mount Aventine: they intended to make this spot the center of a protest against the "Final Act"

wonted: usual

girdle: belt, sash

lay flatling: lay on the ground

People

her brother Crassus: one of the sons of the *Pontifex Maximus*

Historic Occasions

121 B.C.: Opimius was consul along with Quintus Fabius Maximus Allobrogicus

On the Map

Mount Aventine: the Aventine Hill, another of the Seven Hills

Reading

Part One

About that time there happened likewise a difference between Gaius and his fellow-officers, about this occasion. A show of gladiators was to be exhibited before the people in the marketplace, and most of the magistrates erected **scaffolds** round about, to take money for the standing. Gaius commanded them to take them down again, because the poor men might see the sport without any cost. But not a man of them would yield to it. Wherefore he stayed till the night before the pastime should be, and then he took all his labourers he had under him, and went and overthrew the scaffolds every one of them: so that the next morning all the marketplace was clear for the common people to see the pastime at their pleasure. For this fact of his, the people thanked him marvellously, and took him for a worthy man.

Howbeit his brethren the tribunes were very much offended with him, and took him for a bold, **presumptuous** man. This seemeth to be the chief cause why **he was put from his third tribuneship**, where he had the most voices of his side: because his colleagues, out of revenge, caused false **returns** to be made. But as to this matter there was a controversy. Certain it is, he very much resented this repulse, and he behaved with unusual arrogance towards some of his adversaries who were joyful at his defeat, telling them that all this was but a false, **sardonic** mirth, as they little knew how much his actions threw them into obscurity.

As soon as Opimius also was chosen consul, they presently cancelled several of Gaius's laws, and especially called into question his proceedings at Carthage, omitting nothing that was likely to irritate him, that from some effect of his passion they might find out a tolerable pretense to put him to death. Gaius notwithstanding did patiently bear it at the first; but afterwards his friends, and specially Fulvius, did encourage him so, that he began again to gather men to resist the consul. They say also that on this occasion his mother, Cornelia, joined in the sedition, and assisted him by sending privately several strangers into Rome, under pretense as if they came to be hired there for harvest-men; **intimations** of this are given in her letters to him. However, it is confidently affirmed by others that Cornelia did not in the least approve of these actions.

When the day came that they should proceed to the **revocation** of his laws, both parties met by break of day at the Capitol. There when the consul Opimius had done sacrifice, an attendant on the consul, called Quintus Antyllius, carrying the entrails of the beast sacrificed, said unto Fulvius and his friends who stood about him, "Give place to honest men, vile citizens that ye be." Some report that, besides this provoking language, he extended his naked arm towards them, as a gesture of scorn and contempt. Whereupon they slew him presently in the field with great **bodkins to write with**, which they had purposely made for that intent.

Hereupon the common people were marvellously offended for this murder, and the chief men of both sides also were diversely affected. For Gaius was very sorry for it, and bitterly reproved them that were about him, saying that they had given their enemies the occasion they looked for, to set upon them. Opimius, immediately seizing the occasion thus offered, was in great delight, and urged the people to revenge. But there fell a great shower of rain that put an end to the business of that day.

Part Two

Early the next morning, Opimius the consul summoned the Senate, and whilst he advised with the senators in the senate-house, some had taken the body of Antyllius and laid it naked upon the **bier**, and so carried it through the marketplace (as it was agreed upon before amongst them) and brought it to the door of the Senate house, where they began to make great moan and lamentation. Opimius was not at all ignorant that this was designed to be done; however, he seemed to be surprised, and wondered what the meaning of it should be. The senators, therefore, presently went out to know the occasion of it, and, standing about the corpse, uttered exclamations against the inhuman and barbarous act. But on the other side, this did revive the old grudge and malice of the people, for the wickedness of the ambitious noblemen: who having themselves before slain Tiberius Gracchus that was tribune, within the Capitol itself, and had also cast his body into the river, yet now they could honour with their presence and their public lamentations in the Forum the corpse of an ordinary hired attendant (who, though he might perhaps die wrongfully, was, however, in a great measure **the occasion of it himself**), by these means hoping to undermine him who was the only remaining defender and safeguard of the people.

The senators, after some time, withdrew, and presently ordered that Opimius, the consul, should be **invested with extraordinary power** to protect the commonwealth and suppress all tyrants. This being decreed, the consul presently commanded the senators that were present there to go arm themselves, and the Roman knights to be in readiness very early the next morning, and every one of them to be attended with two servants, well-armed.

Fulvius, on the other side, prepared his force against them, and assembled the common people together. Gaius also, returning from the marketplace, made a stop just before his father's statue, and fixing his eyes for some time upon it, remained in a deep contemplation; at length he burst out a-weeping, and fetching a great sigh, went his way. This made no small impression upon those who saw it, and they began to **upbraid** themselves that they should desert and betray so worthy a man as Gaius. They therefore went directly to his house, remaining there as a guard about it all night, though in a different manner from those who were a guard to Fulvius; for they passed away the night with shouting and drinking, and Fulvius himself, being the first to get drunk, spoke and acted many things very unbecoming a man of his age and character.

They that watched Gaius, on the other side, were very sorrowful, and made no noise, even as in a common calamity of their country, devising with themselves what would fall out upon it, waking and sleeping one after another by turns. As soon as daylight appeared, they roused Fulvius, who had not yet slept off the effects of his drinking; and having armed themselves with the weapons hung up in his house, that were formerly taken from the **Gauls**, whom he conquered in the time of his consulship, they presently, with threats and loud acclamations, **made their way towards Mount Aventine**.

But Gaius would not arm himself, but went out of his house in a long gown, as if he would have gone simply into the marketplace according to his **wonted** manner, saving that he carried a short dagger at his **girdle** under his gown. So as he was going out of his house, his wife stayed him at the door, and holding him by the one hand, and a little child of his by her other hand, she said thus unto him:

> "Alas Gaius, thou dost not now go as thou wert
> wont, as a tribune into the marketplace to speak to
> the people, neither to prefer any new laws; neither
> dost thou go unto an honest war, that if
> unfortunately that should happen to thee that is
> common to all men, I might yet at the least mourn
> for thy death with honour. But thou goest to put
> thyself into bloody butchers' hands, who most
> cruelly have slain thy brother Tiberius; and yet thou
> goest, a naked man unarmed, intending rather to
> suffer, than to do hurt. Besides, thy death can bring
> no benefit to the commonwealth. For the worser
> part hath now the upper hand, considering that
> sentence passeth by force of sword...But such may
> be my misfortune, that I may presently go to pray
> the river or sea to give me thy body, which as thy
> brother's they have likewise thrown into the same.
> Alas, what hope or trust is left us now, in laws or
> gods, since they have slain Tiberius?"

As Licinia was making this pitiful moan unto him, Gaius fair and softly pulled his hand from her, and left her, giving her never a word, but went on with his friends. But she reaching after him to take him by the gown, fell to the ground, and **lay flatling** there a great while, speaking never a word: until at length her servants took her up in a swoon, and carried her so unto **her brother Crassus**.

Narration and Discussion

Why did the senators take such extreme measures at this time? What were their worst fears?

Explain how Gaius ended up in such a dangerous position.

Creative narration: William Shakespeare was often inspired by Plutarch, sometimes borrowing whole lines from North's translation. Choose one incident and rewrite it as Shakespeare might have done.

Lesson Twelve

Introduction

Outlawed by the Roman authorities, Gaius and his supporters now had no choice but to fight fiercely for their lives.

Vocabulary

herald's rod: a *cadeuceus*, which was a symbol of peaceful negotiations

committed into custody: jailed

rout: disorderly retreat

Furies: the goddesses of vengeance

did so embrace: held onto him so tightly

jointure: dowry; money paid at one's wedding

Concord: Concordia, the goddess of agreement

infamy: being well known, but not in a good way

Historic Occasions

121 B.C.: Death of Gaius Gracchus

c. 115 B.C.: Death of Cornelia

Reading

Part One

Fulvius, when the people were gathered together in a full body, by the advice of Gaius sent his younger son (which was a pretty fair boy) into the marketplace, with a **herald's rod** in his hand. This boy humbly presenting his duty, with the tears in his eyes, before the consul and Senate, offered them peace. The most of them that were present thought very well of it. But Opimius made answer, saying that it became them not to send messengers, thinking with fair words to win the Senate, but it was their duty to come themselves in persons, like subjects and offenders to make their trial, and so to crave pardon, and to seek to pacify the wrath of the Senate. Then he commanded the boy he should not return again to them unless they would comply with these conditions.

Gaius (as it is reported) was ready to go and clear himself unto the Senate: but none of his friends consented to it. Whereupon Fulvius sent his son back again unto them, to speak for them as he had done before. But Opimius, that was desirous to fight, caused the boy to be taken, and **committed into custody**; and then went presently against Fulvius with a great number of footmen well-armed, and of Cretan archers besides, who with their arrows did more trouble and hurt their enemies than with anything else, so that a **rout** and flight quickly ensued. Fulvius, on the other side, fled into an obscure bathing-house; but shortly after being discovered, he and his eldest son were slain together.

Gaius was not observed to use any violence against anyone; but, extremely disliking all these outrages, retired to the Temple of Diana. There he attempted to kill himself, but was hindered by his faithful friends, Pomponius and Licinius; they took his sword away from him, and counselled him to flee. It is reported that then he fell down on his knees, and holding up both his hands unto the goddess, he besought her that the people might never come out of bondage, to be revenged of this, their ingratitude and treason. For as soon as a proclamation was made of a pardon, the greater part openly deserted him.

Gaius, therefore, endeavoured now to make his escape, but was pursued so close by his enemies, as far as the wooden bridge, that from thence he narrowly escaped. There his two trusty friends begged of him to preserve his own person by flight, whilst they in the meantime would keep their post, and maintain the passage; neither could their enemies, until they were both slain, pass the bridge.

Now there was none that fled with Gaius, but one of his men called Philocrates: notwithstanding, every man did still encourage and counsel him, as they do men to win a game; but no man would help him, nor offer him any horse, though he often required it, because he saw his enemies so near unto him. However, he had still time enough to hide himself in a little grove, consecrated to the **Furies**. In that place, his servant Philocrates having first slain him, presently afterwards killed himself also, and fell dead upon his master. Though some affirm it for a truth, that they were both taken alive by their enemies, and that Philocrates **did so embrace** his master that none of the enemies could strike him for all the blows they gave, before he was slain himself.

[omission for length and content]

Part Two

The bodies of these two men, Gaius Gracchus and Fulvius, and of their other followers (which were to the number of three thousand that were slain), were all thrown into the river, their goods confiscated, and their widows forbidden to put themselves into mourning. They dealt even more severely with Licinia, Caius's wife, and deprived her even of her **jointure**; and as in addition still to all their inhumanity, they barbarously murdered Fulvius's youngest son; his only crime being, not that he took up arms against them, or that he was present in the battle, but merely that he had come with the articles of agreement: for this he was first imprisoned, then slain.

But yet that which most of all other grieved the people, was the Temple of **Concord**, which Opimius caused to be built: for it appeared that he boasted, and in manner triumphed, that he had slain so many citizens of Rome. And therefore somebody in the night time wrote, under the inscription of the temple, these verses:

A furious fact and full of beastly shame.

This temple built, that beareth Concord's name.

Epilogue

This Opimius was the first man at Rome, that, being consul, usurped the absolute power of the dictator; and that without law or justice condemned three thousand citizens of Rome, besides Fulvius Flaccus (who had also been consul, and had received the honour of triumph), and Gaius Gracchus, a young man in like case, who in virtue and reputation excelled all the men of his years. Afterwards he was found incapable of keeping his hands from thieving. For when he was sent as ambassador unto Jugurtha, king of Numidia, he was bribed with money; and thereupon being accused, he was most shamefully convicted, and condemned. Wherefore he ended his days with this reproach and **infamy**, hated, and mocked of all the people; because at the time of the overthrow he dealt beastly with them that fought for his quarrel.

But shortly after, it appeared to the world how much they lamented the loss of the two brethren of the Gracchi. For they made images and statues of them, and caused them to be set up in an open and honourable place, consecrating the places where they had been slain: and many of them also came and offered to them, of their first fruits and flowers, according to the time of the year, and went thither to make their prayers on their knees, as unto the temples of the gods. Their mother Cornelia, as writers report, did bear this calamity with a noble heart: and as for the chapels which they built and consecrated unto them in the place where they were slain, she said no more, but that they had such graves as they had deserved.

Afterwards she dwelt in the city of Misenum, and never changed her manner of life. She had many friends, and because she was a noble lady, and loved ever to welcome strangers, she kept a very good house, and therefore had always great repair unto her of Grecians and learned men: besides, there was no king nor prince, but both received gifts from her, and sent gifts to her again. They that frequented her company, delighted marvellously to hear her report the deeds and manner of her father's life, Scipio Africanus (#1): but yet they wondered more, to hear her tell the acts and death of her two sons, Tiberius and Gaius, without shedding a tear, or making any show of lamentation or grief, no more than if she had told an history unto them that had requested her. Insomuch some writers report, that age, or her great misfortunes, had overcome and taken her reason and sense from her, to feel any sorrow. But indeed they were senseless to say so, not understanding, how that to be nobly born, and virtuously brought up, doth make men temperately to digest sorrow, and though Fortune may often be more successful, and may defeat the efforts of virtue to avert misfortunes, it cannot, when we incur them, prevent our bearing them patiently *[Dryden: reasonably]*.

Narration and Discussion

Opimius refused to negotiate with the "rebels," because "it was their duty to come themselves in persons, like subjects and offenders to make their trial, and so to crave pardon, and to seek to pacify the wrath of the Senate." Do you agree?

Why did Gaius's friends encourage but not help him?

For older students and further thought #1: After this uprising, and the subsequent purge of three thousand people, Roman reaction turned to regret. Two Gracchi brothers put to death by angry mobs seemed like two too many; not to mention the many other lives lost. What impact did they have on the laws of Rome, or on the rights of citizens to have a voice? Were their efforts worth the cost of their lives?

Creative narration: "But shortly after, it appeared to the world how much they lamented the loss of the two brethren of the Gracchi." Expand on this in any way you wish (news interview, editorial, dialogue).

Examination Questions

For younger students:

1. Tell about Tiberius's meeting with the Numantines (there was something he wanted from them).

2. "Cicero the orator also sayeth that Gaius was bent altogether to flee from office in the commonwealth, and to live quietly as a private man." What changed his mind?

For older students:

1. Like his brother before him, Gaius Gracchus sometimes did the right things in wrong ways, or at least in ways that created jealousy or suspicion. Give examples.

2. (High school) "So in a short time he did excel all the young men of his time, as well in obedience as in the valiantness of his person." Who is being described? Did he live up to this early evaluation?

Bibliography

Plutarch's Lives of the Noble Greeks and Romans. Englished by Sir Thomas North. With an introduction by George Wyndham. London: Dent, 1894.

Plutarch's Lives: The Dryden Plutarch. Revised by Arthur Hugh Clough. London: J.M. Dent, 1910.

About the Author

Anne E. White (www.annewrites.ca) is the author of *Minds More Awake: The Vision of Charlotte Mason* and *Ideas Freely Sown: The Matter and Method of Charlotte Mason,* as well as other books in The Plutarch Project series. She is an Advisory member of the AmblesideOnline Curriculum.

www.ingramcontent.com/pod-product-compliance
Lightning Source LLC
LaVergne TN
LVHW051627080426
835511LV00016B/2208